ecstatic

ARCHITECTURE

ecstatic

ARCHITECTURE

The Surprising Link

From a debate of the Academy International Forum at the
Royal Academy

CHARLES JENCKS

ACADEMY EDITIONS

Acknowledgements

This book started life by accident, as an evening's debate at the Royal Academy of Arts. As I mention several times, this discussion was surprisingly pleasant and fruitful, leading to further thoughts and the formation of a new category of discourse: Ecstatic Architecture. Inevitably, then, I am grateful to the architects who took part in these discussions; particularly, Paolo Portoghesi, Nigel Coates, Ron Arad and Robert Maxwell and the organisers of the evening, Mary Ann Stevens, Maggie Toy and the Academy Forum. Portoghesi, as his text shows, also sees the connections between the historic origin of this concept and its present transformations. Frank Gehry, as always, has been an inspiration for some ideas expressed here, and a thoughtful friend. To him and other architects who have given freely of their time and material – Daniel Libeskind, Rem Koolhaas and Will Alsop – I express a deep gratitude. I have also benefited from, and enjoyed, discussions on the subject with Wolfgang Prix. On the editorial side, I would like to thank Maggie Toy and Mariangela Palazzi-Williams for their continued support, and Mario Bettella and Andrea Bettella of Artmedia for designing the book.

Photographic credits

All photographs are courtesy of the architects or from Charles Jencks, unless stated otherwise; every effort has been made to locate sources and credit material but in the very few cases where this has not been possible our apologies are extended: Alsop & Störmer pp109-113; Ron Arad Associates pp120-123; Avincola, Rome p9; Mario Bettella pp78-81, 83, 85; Tom Bonner p43 (top); Branson Coates Architecture pp16, 35 (bottom), 86, 87 (top, middle), 88 (top), 89 (top), 90, 91 (bottom), 92-93, 95 (bottom), 96; Christian Ducker + Nigel Coates p91 (top); G Dagon p124; Fischer von Erlach, Entwurf, 1722 p33; Odile Decq - B Cornette pp114-119; Ned Flex pp87 (bottom), 88 (bottom); FMGB Guggenheim Bilbao Museoa p171; Bruce Goff pp127-129; Eddie Valentine Holmes p89 (bottom); Ariel Huber Studio Libeskind p149 (bottom); Charles Jencks 11-15, 17-19, 24-32, 34, 35 (top) 36, 43 (bottom), 44-55, 66, 126, 130-131, 132 (left), 133-148, 149 (top), 150-154, 155 (bottom), 156, 157 (top), 166, 168-170, 173; C Kicherer pp124-125; OMA p157 (middle); Paolo Portoghesi pp56, 57, 60-65; Reiser + Umemoto p132; Christian Richters p155 (top); Phil Sayers p94; Turkish Embassy, London p20; Philip Vile p95 (top); Gerald Zugmann, pp2, 98-106.

Cover: New Guggenheim Museum, Bilbao, Spain, Frank Gehry, 1993–97; Illustration by Mario Bettella based on an original photograph courtesy of the New Guggenheim Museum, Bilbao
Frontispiece: UFA Cinema Center, Dresden, Germany, Coop Himmelb(l)au, 1993–98
Back cover: Nigel Coates, Millennium Figure for the Dome, London 2000

First published in Great Britain in 1999 by
ACADEMY EDITIONS

A division of
JOHN WILEY & SONS
Baffins Lane
Chichester
West Sussex PO19 1UD

ISBN: 0 471 98398 5

Other Wiley Editorial Offices
New York • Weinheim • Brisbane • Singapore • Toronto

Printed and bound in China

Contents

Ecstatic Architecture – The Surprising Link

Charles Jencks

On 17 November 1997, the Academy Forum at the Royal Academy of Arts in London held one of its recurrent debates on a subject that preoccupies contemporary architects. One pretext for the subject was the *Sensation* exhibition then on show at the Royal Academy and another was the new concept of psychic space engaging architects, variously termed 'Psychological', 'Enchanted' and 'Intangible'. Realising the flatness of these terms, I suggested 'Ecstatic Architecture', and so the evening's agenda was prepared with an historical look at such things as Baroque architecture and the ecstasy of St Teresa – always a touchstone of such mental/physical rapture.

I was sceptical of the word and concept, because they often refer to a dream-like state where conscious control and voluntary will are given over to a semi-automatic response. The users' response to the drug Ecstasy typifies this kind of repetitive, thoughtless behaviour. But on the evening this initial doubt was itself doubted. Nearly everyone taking part in the discussion – and they included some of the warring factions of architecture – warmed to the subject. Somehow the term opened up thought, or at least swept aside the usual mental battle lines that divide architects. Was it that they could talk freely about their deeper motivations without fear of censure or ridicule, or trouble from potential clients? Or even admit to non-functional desires? Or was it something internal to the concept of ecstasy which uncovered some previously hidden meanings in architecture?

Whatever the case the evening was a surprise, and 'Ecstatic

Architecture' continues to surprise me. It may illuminate a lot more architecture than we think, and here it is used in a somewhat extended way which has roots in its historic past, *ekstasis* εκστασισ. The fruitfulness of a concept lies partly in the breadth of new material it brings together in a new light. Ecstatic Architecture has allowed us to think about buildings widely distant in function and time, from cave art to the New Guggenheim Museum in Bilbao, from explicitly erotic architecture and objects to buildings which have a spiritual role, from conceptual and cybernetic artefacts to pure architecture. It is a concept which allows us comparisons that might have been overlooked: between the current practice of leading architects such as Frank Gehry, Coop Himmelb(l)au, Nigel Coates and historic architecture. The surprise is that Ecstatic Architecture has brought together these widely divergent strands. The spiritual, erotic and emphatically material motives in architecture have an unlikely link and here they are looked at jointly and reconsidered in a new key.

Ecstatic Architecture may induce a sense of euphoria, or be part of a ritual experience meant to do so, or it may arouse a sense of devotion, awe, love and deeper understanding; or it may through aesthetic and conceptual means excite the more purely architectural passions. As this variety shows, it does not have a single motive, but it certainly aims at inclusion and a unitive experience which is why, like creativity itself, it brings together into a new whole such disparate material.

Ecstatic Architecture
Charles Jencks

For two days and nights we had been working, my friends and I, high on ideas and lack of sleep, feverishly filling our walls with cigarette ash and the haze of spray-gun-mist. We felt trapped in the icy frigidity of a Mod-Con overlooking the false Eros, when suddenly we heard, spreading over the city, the reverberent sounds of the velvet underground amplified across the neon, flowing across every solid structure like viscous steel, crossing every boundary, uniting every category in a vortex of movement . . . We reached for our liquid guns and plastic fur and started up, erect as a new breed of creators, armed with the latest technology and began to spray new enticing shapes never seen before – torus, tornado, whirlpool, cantilevered curls . . . I bounced my nude body from one pneumatic structure to the next oblivious to all right-angled boredom and, filled with the superior knowledge of quantum physics and neuro-transmitters, merged suddenly with the others . . . Together we activated brain-cells, the superorganism which like a vacuum in outer space lifted us beyond the confines of a heavy architecture and our bodies. I flung my senses across the artificial landscape of synthetic fur and pulsating mounds and, wafted by all the neurotransmitters we reached that moment of bliss which is Pure Architecture, the orgasmic oneness of cantilevered movement, the vertical lift-off, the derangement of senses . . . floating, floating, floating, disembodied like Yuri in outer space without weight or centre . . . Point 5) We demand a synthetic fur and melting ice, a 2nd Nature moulded to our bodies, dissolving crystals always changing and as responsive to our desires as a friendly dog.

These lines, from the little-known *Fur and Ice Manifesto*, 1968, name virtually all the qualities of Ecstatic Architecture – the emphasis on new technologies of bliss, the overcoming of habitual categories of experience, the belief in a new science of transcendence, and a series of metaphors of ecstasy. Movement, lift-off, the cantilever – the desire for out-of-body architecture that reaches heavenwards – and new means of achieving this state: neon, music, drugs, slippery materials that unite all surfaces and especially spray-on fur that make them comfortable. The fashion for new super material like structural fur and viscous steel dates this manifesto to the time of *Barbarella*, the film starring Jane Fonda, who slithered around and merged with the sensuous environment. There is the passing reference to the Russian cosmonaut, Yuri Gagarin, the first man in outer space, the first to have a real disembodied experience achieved through high-technology. Zero-gravity, polymorphous sex also marks it as a 1960s fantasy and we can place its origin near, or overlooking Piccadilly Circus because of the clear reference to neon and the 'false Eros', shooting its arrow into the ground ('Shafts-Bury Square').

The manifesto clearly contrasts the new consciousness with the old – an out-of-body experience with the weightiness of Modern building ('right-angled boredom'). Missing, inevitably, from this corpus is the 1990s drug, Ecstasy, and other contemporary techniques of computer simulation which allow a viscous architecture to be built today, but in most respects it is surprisingly up-to-date and prescient. In spite of its sub-Futurist rhetoric (which also dates it to the late-1960s) the question it poses for this book, as well as for architectural history in general, is about the nature of styles and cultural events: what kind of genre is Ecstatic Architecture? Is it a distinct time-bound movement or a transhistorical category? Is it a 1990s fashion suitable to the deranged mood of the *Fin de Millennium* or something of an eternal dream (one going back to Ancient Greece)?

Most architectural movements can be divided into two types, those which are loosely organised and implicitly related, such as Art Nouveau, and those which are explicitly defined by leaders and followers, such as De Stijl. Ecstatic Architecture is definitely of the first type and hence the term is open to question. Perhaps other concepts are more suitable, and contenders for the title have been Psychological Architecture, Intangible Architecture, Enchanted Space, Excessive Architecture, Euphoric Architecture – appellations which have to be considered. They fail, however descriptively accurate, because they are all relatively anodyne.

But whichever term is adopted, we must keep in mind the global condition to which it refers. There *is* something going on which crosses the usual categories and divisions of the design world, and it needs definition regardless of the one-liner we choose. An approach exists which focuses on the architectural language itself, intensifying it to the point that we may become bewildered, disoriented, thrown off balance. *Ek-stasis*, from the Ancient Greek, means 'to put out of place', 'to drive a person out of his wits' and in Late Greek it came to mean 'withdrawal of the soul from the body into a mystic trance', a meaning it keeps today. Ecstatic prophecy was a common condition for Hebrew prophets, and several means were developed to induce a trance such as dancing, starvation, whirling in a circle, reciting repetitive chants, or perhaps even the non-canonic getting drunk. (Sexual-religious ecstasy, although the obvious deep metaphor which has remained in the back of everyone's mind for perhaps 50,000 years, was not allowed to come to the fore.) Particularly, *architectural* ecstasy was rare: St Simon Stylites sitting alone in the desert atop his column; a foreigner entering the Pantheon in Rome, confronted for the first time with the spinning coffers and exploding glare of the oculus; any of the Seven Wonders of the World. While extraordinary architecture has always had an ecstatic component, we are concerned here with the way intentions to overwhelm, stupefy and seduce have become motives for both commercial and serious architects today – and some artists.

The exhibition *Sensation* at the Royal Academy of Arts, in the autumn of 1997, raises the question of how far the accentuation of the sensual and the sensational can legitimatise a work of art, and 'Ecstatic Space', an evening's debate at the same place during this exhibition, raised

Gian Lorenzo Bernini, The Ecstasy of St Teresa, *and Cornaro Chapel, Santa Maria della Vittoria, Rome, 1645–52. The blank exterior, with its cantilevered box allowing interior, indirect lighting, is an early example of black-box architecture: the dumb outside contrasts with the controlled media on the inside. This presents, in a warm glowing light, the moment when the saint is about to be pierced by a fiery arrow of divine love. Her body and skirts ascend in a billowing cloud and her orgasmic mood is taken up in every detail including the polished, flowing marble. This overpowering unity of mood typifies Ecstatic Architecture, as does the weightlessness, ascension, empathetic use of shiny materials and facial expression. Bernini's work remains the touchstone of the genre*

similar questions for architecture. This, in turn, stimulated some of the essays in this volume and provided the pretext for a book to explore this hidden genre. (There is an argument that ecstasy is more ecstatic when imperfectly understood.)

In the past, as Paolo Portoghesi's essay makes clear, Baroque and Rococo architects sought a sensuality in building, particularly when they were designing churches. Francesco Borromini and Balthasar Neumann dematerialised matter by mixing forms, crossing shapes, and exploding them with light. This created a disorientation, a confusion of senses, which is essential to *ek-stasis* and, inevitably, upsetting to normal, Protestant rationalists, which is why it was roundly condemned in Britain for the next two hundred years. *The Ecstasy of St Teresa* by Gian Lorenzo Bernini was meant to induce an ecstatic state in the onlooker, not just to represent a passionate moment. The excess of accentuated slippery surfaces and various architectural devices – such as the manipulation of mysterious light and space – were sanctioned by religious convention. In the Rococo churches of the Asam brothers and Balthasar Neumann, the sensation is of being either in a celestial elevator or an ethereal boudoir. Heaven or sex. The two have been connected as a common form of transcendence since at least the time of the Ancient Greeks.

It is interesting that the architecture of pleasure, or the pleasure of architecture, has become an identifiable genre in the 1990s, a transformation of previous positions. Partly this is a consequence of the excesses of a consumer society, as Nigel Coates mentions, citing the notorious French philosopher Jean Baudrillard's view of the Post-Modern world: 'We live in the ecstasy of communication. And this ecstasy is obscene'. The excess of advertisement dominates both the high street and the media; beyond these are the dislocated cyberspaces of young designers, the fantasy sets for Michael Jackson and MTV, and a particular tradition of interior design that can be traced back to 1960s Italy, of *La Dolce Vita* and Supersensualism. Many of these environments and images are persuasive and are meant to overpower us with confusion, with a loss of boundaries and with a surfeit of sensual detail. Moralists condemn (or celebrate) the genre, as Arthur Kroker and David Cook have done in their *The Postmodern Scene, Excremental Culture and Hyperaesthetics,* 1986. Excess and ecstasy have their carnal sides and these break boundaries.

Gruppo Strum (Ceretti, Derossi and Rosso), Pratone ('Big Meadow'), Milan, 1970. The Italian Supersensualists, in the late 1960s, satirised and exploited images of consumption, sensuality and youth culture. Ek-stasis, 'to be put out of place', has always meant a mystifying dislocation and here, as the laughing actress falls about, one wonders what is being sold – a seat, a bed, or a big meadow of squashy leaves? (Courtesy the architects)

Coop Himmelb(l)au, Exhibition Space, New Groningen Museum, 1996. Exploding, dissolving space, like the anti-gravity architecture of Zaha Hadid, dissolves boundaries, mixes categories and confuses the senses. Disorientation used positively has always been a method of Ecstatic Architecture, but few have used it as rhetorically as the architects known as 'Blue Sky'

In the architectural world, Coop Himmelb(l)au explodes space apart with such a frenzy of conflicting cues that we are forced to experience it aesthetically. Wolf Prix, founder of this group, has sung the pleasures of a chaotic, polymorphous architecture since the late 1960s and his cloud projects are moving projects which shift under their own weight, respond and melt away like clouds ('Himmelblau' as 'Blue Sky'). 'Architecture is the black hole in the universe,' he says. 'A lot of gravity but no ground.' He wishes to extend the project of the Tower of Babel – against divine order – by increasing the confusion of architectural tongues because therein lies liberation, the pluralism of cities. His 'liquid space', 'dissolving facades', and a grammar of cantilevers, vectors and tangents are perhaps as close to complete chaos as the Expressionist wing of ecstasy can get. Daniel Libeskind drew various exploding cocktails, such as *Maldoror's Equation* in the late 1970s, and Marcos Novak has represented even greater complexities through computer simulation in his hypersurfaces of the late 1990s, but Coop Himmelb(l)au has actually managed to have such explosions built. The unabashed celebration of unusable, impossible space, space dedicated solely to the joy of architecture, put them squarely in the E-Tradition. How can one experience the pleasure of such things without abandonment? If the explosion of space and light is meant to be overwhelming, it is hard, even pointless, to try to hold on to the usual anchors of orientation, the Cartesian grid. That would be like walking in outer space expecting gravity to apply – possible, but counter-productive; a misunderstanding, a category mistake. One enters a fun-house with sloping floor, or the tilted house in the garden at Bomarzo, knowing that disorientation and feeling sick are appropriate. Architecture, like literature, asks for a willing suspension of disbelief so that, like the reader, the viewer can enter a virtual world (not the world of virtuality).

THE EXCESS OF THE AVANT-GARDE

Today some highly visible international designers have emerged who self-consciously exaggerate the self-referential nature of the architectural sign. A short-list would include Frank Gehry, Eric Moss, Morphosis, Zaha Hadid, Philippe Starck, Shin Takamatsu, Alessandro Mendini, Peter Eisenman, Rem Koolhaas, Nigel Coates, William Alsop, Odile Decq, Jean Nouvel and Ron Arad. They share neither style nor ideology although they

Jean Nouvel, Galleries Lafayette, Berlin, 1993–96. The sensuous meeting of commerce, a see-through emporium and a cosmic concetto. One looks through the department store at different levels of consumption and eating and begins to understand the pervasive metaphor, that shopping has become a form of transcendent religion, from Black Hole to Heaven – one continuous, disorienting, slippery space

are motivated partly by both. More clearly, they are united in the single-minded pursuit of their personal ideas of architecture – a desire to impress and persuade through architecture – and the international information network. They are also driven by a strong will to create artful form, a *Kunstwollen*. They often appear on the same architectural competition short-lists, where their designs provide a sensual element within a formal rhetoric.

NEW BUILDING TASKS

There are other kinds of question to be asked. Why should a type of architecture, dominated by 'boutique architects' (as they are sometimes dismissively known) have emerged? Partly, no doubt, it responds to new building types and the demands of a new audience seeking a different spatial experience: nightclubs such as the Ministry of Sound in London; small shops and restaurants which have to compete through excessive styling; large department stores; light and sound shows; raves and music festivals. Should one attribute this architectural development either to consumer society or to the 'ecstasy of communication', the way signs in a mediascape take on their own new rhetoric? Such questions also reveal the dark side of Ecstatic Architecture, its occasionally manipulative nature, its deceit and cynicism, its subservience to power and money (tendencies shared by the Baroque). Persuasion and rhetoric can be co-opted as well as co-opt.

LIBERATION AND BILBAOISM

Among serious architects the new genre partly reflects an exhaustion with the traditional ideologies of Functionalism, Urbanism, Technism and even the usual norms that drive capitalist society – beliefs in progress, community values and ecological concerns. Architects and the public are tired of these justifications or, perhaps more to the point, suspicious of the way they have been abused; few believe that they are really why an architect designs in a certain way. The variety of choices facing architects in a consumer society challenges such explanations. At the Academy symposium I was surprised that the concept of Ecstatic Architecture was accepted so readily and uncritically, but perhaps the reason is that the term acknowledges the highly personal motivations which often lie behind building. For some it may even legitimise personal expression and be a more

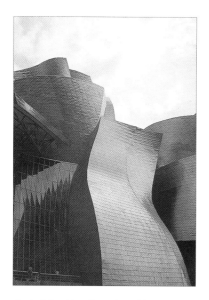

Frank Gehry, New Guggenheim Museum, Bilbao, 1993–97. Architecture compellingly referring to its own plane of expression has become the leading form of Ecstatic Architecture and its exemplar is now so well known and successful as to initiate the category – 'Bilbaoism'

honest indicator of artistic motivations. In this sense the concept may liberate formal invention, become a licence to throw off false strictures, self-imposed taboos.

Admission of visual preference, or acknowledging the dreams and contingencies behind design, has become more acceptable and relevant to the art of architecture. Aesthetic choice, for itself and its internal world, has become more prevalent today and so too the notion that pleasure is its own reward. Frank Gehry's Bilbao overwhelms taboos, not through argument but through architectural rhetoric, a situation which, because of the media celebration throughout the world, could be called 'Bilbaoism'. The New Guggenheim Museum may have all sorts of important justifications such as regenerating a city, or celebrating the role of culture today, but it is quite obvious that the building succeeds for another reason. It celebrates the art of architecture for itself, and it does this to excess, by multiplying the titanium panel for all-over use, by creating vast stretches of unusable, whirling, vortexing space, by undulating over and through the city (beneath expressways) like a viscous steel dragon.

Of course all artistic languages focus on the expressive plane and that is what defines them as art: the aesthetic sign is always self-reflexive. However, it is the *degree* to which this work heightens the artistic sign, its excess and obviousness, which mark it as Ecstatic Architecture and which also defines the sub-genre of Bilbaoism. If in kitsch 'nothing succeeds like excess' the same is often true with ecstasy because excess induces a trance-like state in the onlooker. When one walks through the Bilbao Museum the tactile and spatial effects are so overwhelming they dominate over the experience of art: they heighten the art, it is true, and transport it to a vertiginous, dizzying climax. The curious paradox of Ecstatic Architecture is that, when it is good enough, its self-referentiality becomes extra-referential, universal, transcendent. This can happen even when it is anti-social, anti-nature, anti the public realm, although it gains immeasurably by having an ulterior purpose.

A TYPOLOGY?

Ecstatic Architecture, or the 'E-word' as it was quickly dubbed at the Royal Academy symposium, has some shared tropes and desires which make it a coherent tradition. Paolo Portoghesi mentions the will to movement,

Ron Arad, Mirror Tables, *inside Jean Nouvel's Cartier Centre, Paris, 1994. Polished mirror tables hover weightlessly in space cutting figures in two and providing further ambiguous reflections for Nouvel's transparent planes*

deviation, shifting and amazement presented by forms that rise, explode and shift elastically. If possible they aspire to heaven or, if not, they aspire to cantilever over the earth – Zaha Hadid's anti-gravitational architecture. These motives and types might be characterised as a search for the infinite and boundless. Nigel Coates mentions the will to frenzy, rapture and dynamic movement; a slippage between categories, a metamorphosis, even a desire to consume the city as a sensual body – 'Ecstacity' (his coinage, though Portoghesi mentioned an earlier one). And Coates also sees an elastic formal system as presenting these possibilities, the metamorphosis of one form into another, such as his Oyster House (page 16). The ultimate desire, perhaps doomed to failure in this static, recalcitrant art, is *to be* the city in evolution, in a process of heterogeneous, riotous unfolding. These motives could be called transgressive.

Finally, there are the psychological states sought in religious and sexual ecstasy, the desire for out-of-body experience, pure sensation in the mind, or the floating experience achieved either by an extended orgasm or the marinating of the brain by activating chemicals common to it. Drugs are the easy and dangerous way. Perhaps the hardest is that mentioned by Umberto Eco in his discussion of the ecstatic kabbala, or

Nigel Coates, Oyster House (for the Ideal Home Exhibition, London, 1998). Cantilevers, tilted walls on the top floor, continuous liquid space and shiny surfaces – many of the hallmarks of Ecstatic Architecture, but now aimed at the mass market. (Courtesy the architect)

kabbala of names. This tradition, starting somewhere between the second and sixth century when the *Sefer Yezirah* or *Book of Creation* was written, becomes more formalised by the thirteenth century, as Eco explains in his *The Search for the Perfect Language* (1994). According to this, God created the world and the words of Hebrew, and even its letters, so that there were some perfect correlations between language and reality. The adept, who was trained in deciphering and performing this language to reveal its hidden correspondences, could achieve an ecstatic state by decomposing and permutating all the elements of the Hebrew Bible into new, sacred meanings. Each letter of YHWH, for instance, could be turned about back to front and rolled like a wheel until it revealed another aspect of divine wisdom. Combined with special techniques of breathing and reciting, this process might result in religious ecstasy, the drunken orgy of significance open to those who believe God created an infinitude of meanings pointing to the same message, the universe as a place of wisdom and rapture. The words, the letters, the language were not just representations of this reality but, as the Bible stated, the actual creative act.

This idea finds an echo in architectural language. If Plato had said 'God is the great architect of all things' and if architects have been searching for a perfect language of expression – which will solve a function and actualise appropriate feelings – then architectural ecstasy should be possible too. It would be the perfect, seamless correspondence between form and function, inducing the right feeling that corresponds to a particular use. No doubt, we think that this perfect language exists when a building is faultless and induces the appropriate feelings, although it is clear that opposite architectural languages may also achieve the same feelings. In this sense Ecstatic Architecture is not only a transhistorical category, it is above all a psychological one.

SPEED

By the same token 'Erotic Architecture', as the Spanish architect Oriol Bohigas once called it, is not sexually provocative, in fact it is not really sexual at all. Rather, it is enigmatic, haptic, bodily engaging and something that 'tickles the fancy'. It also may be designed and built at speed, with the energy of a sketch, jumping, as Philippe Starck says, from concept to finished item in the shortest possible time – 'Because you must not lose

Philippe Starck, exhibition techniques, New Groningen Museum, 1995 – suggestive veiling, movable display units on wheels, porcelain placed underground (as if in the sea) – techniques to create a theatrical mood for displaying treasures found under the sea

Rem Koolhaas, Congres-Expo Stairway and triple height space, Lille, 1993–94. Columns, walls and railings tilt and zigzag, a mirror-finished metal glistens and distorts the space (Duchamp's Nude Descending the Staircase), materials and forms break through each other to create the ecstatic disorientation of large crowds rushing up to visit a mass spectacle – Koolhaas, like Gehry, keeps the energy of the sketch in his method of building at speed

the violence, the passion of the idea'. Gehry and Koolhaas achieve this savageness when, in their best work, they retain a quality of the sketch. Possibly such architecture should not be probed too deeply because, as T S Eliot said of poetry, it is often best appreciated when not fully understood. *Le plaisir du texte* is grasped fleetingly. However, ecstatic space produces the greatest ecstasy when it is in the service of a persuasive role that is public and credible: the background for a museum or a church, the setting for music or a mystical experience. Only the rarest of architects can produce architectural ecstasy from the formal spaces themselves.

The question is: how well does the E-word illuminate a present trend? Judging by its initial reception, the term is helpful rather in the manner of a suggestive Rorschach figure. It is something architects and the public can project on to personally motivated work to give it a poetic freedom, and a relief from dead strictures. In its frank admission of an undefined aesthetic drive, it achieves a certain honesty and allows certain things to be said and done. No doubt it will not last for long – one cannot be in a state of ecstasy except for short moments and those moments must be convincing, which they rarely are – but the concept reveals a partial temper of our times.

POSSIBILITIES AND FAILURES

To gain an idea of the heterogeneity of the practice of Ecstatic Architecture across cultures we have included a critical photographic essay which traces the wide tradition from ancient Classicism through Baroque Rome to Southern Germany, Art Nouveau and today's architects. Essays by architects and critics follow this section to underscore what is being thought about the tradition in the 1990s. Transcripts from the evening at the Royal Academy show, surprisingly, that the term is accepted for contemporary re-use. Five of the main protagonists, and their major projects, flesh out the concept and show it to be a reality deserving respect. There is, inevitably, the darker side.

Las Vegas, in both its commercial and creative moments, spans the gamut from the stereotypical to the hysterical, the silly to the delirious. As for stereotype and reduction, the pill Ecstasy reminds one that the genre can induce a repetitive, monotonous behaviour, if not, as La Vegas often seems, death by cliché. Now international corporations such as NIKE create

Michael Graves, Disney Headquarters, Burbank, California, 1992–93. Michael Eisner and Disney turned Entertainment Architecture, as they called it, into a commercial success with Michael Graves and Robert Stern receiving most of the plum commissions. Here the Seven Dwarfs support the corporation, as they do, an ironic comment on American culture as well as historic caryatids such as those of Giulio Romano. Commercial ersatz, when it is not tamed by corporate respectability, can be wildly creative and does give rise to much ecstatic roadside architecture

1 For a discussion of the San artists see Brian Fagan, *From Black Land to Fifth Sun, The Science of Sacred Sites*, Addison-Wesley (Reading, Ma), 1998, chapter 3

ecstatic environments to induce a lightness of being that sells a lightness of product. Branding by architecture goes along with this formula mixing high-tech, sportswear, glamour and media-bombardment.

The greatest exploitation of Ecstatic Architecture is that called Entertainment Architecture created by Disneyworld, buildings which are neither very entertaining nor architecture, but an ersatz of both. In this environment it is safety, predictability and a substitute for experience which are valued more highly than taking leave of one's senses. It has to be said, however, that the controlled, theatrical space of Disneyworld – where real criminals and orgasms are not allowed – does provide the necessary ease and relaxation without which an ecstatic experience is very hard to achieve. That quality is only possible if the ambience is expansive and consistent enough to induce an overwhelming, sustained mood. Frank Gehry's New Guggenheim Museum at Bilbao is the obvious example, and touchstone of the movement, so it ends the book.

DEEPER MOTIVATIONS

The desire to communicate a transcendent mood, or overpowering experience, has recurred in several periods of architecture. Often the motivations are spiritual and may be directly connected with religious rites and socially induced mystical experience. In prehistoric cultures, shamans led a group performance which had as its goal identification with other-worldly forces, the powers behind nature. It is a plausible supposition that Cro-Magnon cultures, in such places as the caves of Lascaux and Chauvet, created this art in such a context. We surmise this because of so many parallels with surviving cultures based on hunting and gathering.

One such culture is that of the San people of southern Africa (sometimes, pejoratively, called Bushmen). These tribes, whose ancestors have inhabited the Kalahari Desert of Botswana for 10,000 years, still practise a form of mystical art that is meant to link the real and supernatural worlds. San rock art resembles that of Lascaux in that it depicts large animals being hunted, led and charmed by figures dressed as half-animal. In one cave men have attached a rope to the nose of a rain-making animal and they are shown leading it over parched ground to break the drought.[1] Medicine men, according to indigenous informants, first have to charm the dangerous animal with sweet smelling herbs, before starting the rain-making ceremony.

Gian Lorenzo Bernini, The Ecstasy of St Teresa, *Cornaro Chapel, Santa Maria della Vittoria, Rome, 1645–52*

In another rock shelter shamans are shown during a trance performance bleeding from the nose. Apparently, when the antelope they depend on, the eland, is hunted down it too trembles in its death throes, its mouth opens wide and fat gushes from the nostrils. This sign of death and potency is stylised both in the art and in the ritual. More public performances, which include both shaman and tribe, result in rhythmic dancing and hyperventilation. Then a trance is induced, not by hallucinogens but by intense concentration: on the rhythmical music, the work of art and the object of performance – the script, as it were.

Characteristically, the performers cover their hands with paint and repeatedly touch significant parts of a painting. In this way, coupled with the dancing and singing, the potency of the eland is transferred from the image to the performer. This is typical. One finds many such hand images, both layered on top of each other and singular, not only in San art, but at Lascaux and in the art of the American Southwest (see page 28).

No doubt all Ecstatic Architecture aspires to the condition of transcending everyday experience. In the West, the Baroque period was the last time such motivations had a religious sanction. Indeed, for Christianity Bernini's depiction of St Teresa's ecstasy has never been equalled in terms of theatricality and the skill with which several media are combined. Yet, as opposed to San art, one does not imagine Catholic priests engaged in an empathetic mimesis of the image. St Teresa's figure may have suggested levitation to the believer, but she was not meant to induce a corresponding act in public.

Today, Ecstatic Architecture does not have an explicit religious or ritualistic function. Ceremony and performance are not ordinarily tied directly into a building and its iconography, as they were in Egyptian temples. Nevertheless, the desire remains for an architecture that lifts one out of one's skin, and architects are taking notice. Visitors to Frank Gehry's New Guggenheim Museum in Bilbao do not fail to respond to its rhetoric, and the strength of their response shows how much the desire for transcendence remains a potent force in architecture. Culture is no substitute for religion, an art opening is not a spiritual ritual, but Ecstatic Architecture, which appeals to the mind and senses, is as healthy as ever.

Whirling dervishes, Konya, Turkey

Defining Ecstasy

Charles Jencks

How is ecstasy defined? Usually as a mental and physical state of frenzy, rapture, awe, and disembodied transcendence – the mind and spirit on a high. But as a state of mind it varies with the context. A feeling of bliss typifies religious ecstasy, and also the strong sense that one relates to the wholeness and substance of all things. Physical and mental identification, transference, empathy. This mood overlaps with sexual ecstasy, which no doubt engenders an even greater sense of physical relatedness but, to point out the obvious, sexual rapture is usually more active than a religious swoon. Trance, whether through drugs or induced mentally, is a similar state, as is the euphoria generated by rhythmical dancing and hyper-ventilation. Whirling dervishes from Turkey induce a state of dizzy rapture even in spectators and that sense of giddy delight is also achieved by anti-gravitational architecture – cantilevers, towers, rockets.

Chemical neurotransmitters that the body produces naturally also modulate feelings related to ecstasy, as can orgasm. Common to both these chemically induced states and ecstasy are two feelings: that of free-floating pleasure, an out-of-body experience, and an holistic mood. Partly the holism stems from the continuity built into the nervous system, its inertia. The well-known 'Waterfall Illusion' illustrates this. Look at a waterfall for thirty seconds very intensely, then look away and you will see the illusion of the landscape moving, not down but up. The same illusion of reversed movement occurs when one stares at the ground from a moving train and then looks away. The nervous system assumes that information flow will continue in a certain direction, and in ecstatic experience this assumption is turned into a very strong, positive feedback. The conse-quences for architecture are these. To be in a receptive state for an ecstatic experience, one must control the ambience so that the continuity of mood is assured and the person is relaxed, confident, willing to participate and not be disturbed by conflicting cues or information. The holism demands such a controlled, integrated environment and that is why, from the Egyptian temple to the Rococo church to Gehry's all-over titanium at Bilbao a sustained, all-embracing mood is characteristic of Ecstatic Architecture. This holism and totality of design are also characteristic of Fascist architecture and advertisement; but then nothing that is powerful and enjoyable in culture is without its dangers.

The Drug Ecstasy

'What wild ecstasy', Keats writes, and indeed the mood is often frenzied and out of control. For the early Greeks *ekstasis* meant to 'drive a person out of his wits', 'insanity' and 'bewilderment'. Later Greek writers, however, saw the transcendent possibilities, the take-off of the mind from the body. As they define it, *ekstasis* is the 'withdrawal of the soul from the body, mystic or prophetic trance'. Milton's expression of a religious trance and vision typifies this second meaning: 'Dissolve me into ecstasies, And bring all Heaven before mine eyes'. Since, in the West, reason and self-control were valued above passion and prophecy it is not surprising that most uses of the word are negative and refer to pathological states of unconsciousness and catalepsy. The seventeenth-century scholar Robert Burton in his *Anatomy of Melancholy* (1621) explicitly connected opium use with the state of ecstasy and even today there is a school of thought that sees some early religious views, such as that of the Hebrew prophets, as inspired by drug-induced visions.

The drug Ecstasy targets a neurotransmitter system known as 5-HT or serotonin that derives from the brain stem. It floods this part of the brain with much more serotonin than is naturally present, and this produces changes in metabolism and body temperature accompanied by feelings of elation. We do not know, and perhaps never will understand, how an experience correlates with a drug.[1] If the ecstatic mood can be induced through the mind by, among other things, receptivity to ideas, the process of contemplation, the practice of ritual and the appreciation of architecture – that is, top-down – it can also be partly generated through the drug – bottom-up. When both are combined, as in sexual activity enhanced by drugs, the mixture is even more powerful. At least that is true if it is accompanied by a scenario and experienced by those who are

1 S Greenfield, *The Human Brain, A Guided Tour,* Weidenfeld & Nicolson (London), 1997, p89

skilled in such things. The popular writer on sex, drugs and the occult, Robert Anton Wilson, argues convincingly that there are really three things involved, not just the brain and the drug, but also self-programming or traditional guides.

> **Sensations of pleasure [when combining sexual activity and drugs] expand to more areas of the body than usual. One is 'floating' or 'high'. If one is self-programming the trip, via one of Dr. Leary's manuals or the rituals of some older occult tradition, the 'astral' or hallucinatory stage soon begins: the lady may give forth a divine effulgence, a light that seems cosmic and eternal – this is the meaning of Aleister Crowley's mantra 'Every man and every woman is a star' – or, perhaps, she may appear covered with jewels or flowers. With real luck and some skill at self-hypnosis (or real magical ability, as true believers would say) a 'peak experience' will occur shortly before orgasm. This is the terminology that Dr. Abraham Maslow uses and, like similar terms from other sources (Freud's 'oceanic experience', the *satori* of Zen Buddhism, the Hindu 'samadhi', Gurdjieff's 'waking up' etc.), it is difficult to define. It is simply the experience of total ecstasy, usually involving a paradoxical sensation that the whole universe is actually your own body.**[2]**

2   Robert Anton Wilson, *Sex and Drugs, A Journey Beyond Limits* (1973), republished New Falcon Publications (Phoenix, Arizona) 1987, pp14–16. For the recent view that ecstatic experience differs somewhat even in its unitive dimension, see Dan Merkur, *The Ecstatic Imagination, Psychedelic Experiences and the Psychoanalysis of Self-Actualisation*, SUNY (New York), 1998, pp92–95

While this feeling of what is now often called a 'unitive phenomenon' may look the same or similar in its emphasis on holism, more recent scholars now stress the individual and cultural differences which underlie ecstasy.

What is common to both the drug-induced euphoria and ecstatic experience is the continuity and holism of the mood. Also shared is the repetitive behaviour characteristic of ritual and rhythmical dancing and this may partly explain why so much Ecstatic Architecture makes use of hypnotically repeated elements, rhythmical ornament and stereotype. It certainly explains the control and all-pervasive ambience necessary for the experience. All Ecstatic Architecture tends towards the *Gesamtkunstwerk*, the total work of art, where every element joins in the dominant theme and every contradiction is present ultimately to return to and reaffirm the central pattern.

Forms of Ecstasy – Part I *Charles Jencks*
ECSTASY AND NATURE

Metaphors are taken from nature's moods, the qualities which are continuous with us. Nature is often preferred to culture as a place apart, of otherness, and therefore endlessly open to interpretation and new use. Is it a surprise to find it the focus of rapture and awe, the setting and standard for ecstasy, or the place that lovers inevitably seek? Niagara Falls and the Grand Canyon have so often been perceived as climactic expressions of nature in tumultuous ecstasy that they are taken in before they are seen. Paradoxically this works. Anticipation and conventional views keep the experience focused and since rapture also makes use of stereotype, this control actually can reinforce enjoyment.

Grand Canyon, Arizona

Canyon de Chelly,
American Southwest,
Four Corners

On the other hand, less known conjunctions of nature and culture accentuate the savageness behind both and thereby heighten ecstasy. The Canyon de Chelly, in Southwest America, has many habitable perches nestled into the rock face by the Anasazi Indians. The remains of these are set off by violently jagged cliffs and weathered planes, signs of cosmic activity and death. The Ajanta caves in India exaggerate these contrasts even further. Delicate carving and protective enclosure are juxtaposed to a massive brutality: the wandering, fractured joints between nature and culture become the focus. Chinese scholar rocks also play on these contrasts, and so rhetorically that the boundaries between beauty and ugliness, pleasure and pain, are erased as they are in an ecstatic frenzy.

Cave at Ajanta, India

Crystal Cascade (rock design by Charles Jencks)

Gardens and fountains also drama-
tise this point of change-over. At
Bomarzo the most effective
moments are when one is surprised
and mystified. When the bushes
and trees had overgrown the giants
and fantastic animals, they became
even more disquieting. Wilderness
as a sign of abandonment to natural
forces is turned into a high art by
Bernini's sculptures and the giant
gushing fountains in Rome and
Caserta. White marble figures jumping through the foam have been a
cliché of ecstasy since the seventeenth-century, a point reaffirmed
today in holiday advertisements.

Since nature is fecund, polymorphous and variegated, it inevitably
breaks down customary boundaries,
and thus gardens have always been
a place set apart for unexpected
conjunctions and unusual behaviour:
taking leave of your senses through
heightening the senses.

Bomarzo Garden, near
Viterbo, Italy, 1525–75
– Battle of the Titans

G Bernini, Fontana del
Tritone, Rome, 1637

N. Salvi, Trevi Fountain, Rome, 1732–62

Luigi Vanvitelli and others, Cascade and Nymphs, Caserta, Italy, 1752–73

In prehistoric cultures there is no great differentiation between art, magic, ritual and cosmic celebration. The universe is understood as a continuum, and animism pervades it. Everything is potentially alive or empowered and perceived as having a character, a state of mind and sometimes even a soul. The metaphorical imagination is at its height, meanings are transferred from one area to another, the world is partly enchanted. Bodily metaphors are projected on to inanimate objects and places in the landscape that are impressive: large rocks, mountains, caves and forests. In a sense that we will see later this is the start of architectural poetics, the discovery of qualities in the environment.

Rituals mediate between this world and the supernatural. Shamans, often artists as well, lead the tribe in collective performance using potent symbols and sympathetic magic the purpose of which is to restore an harmonious relationship with nature. Healing, hunting, rain-making are some immediate goals, while making the cosmos ordered and fecund are the larger spiritual ends. With historical cultures, such as the Egyptians, all this is systema-tised under a pharaoh and priestly class. Regular, repetitive architecture takes on a ritualistic role in ordering the liturgy.

Pictographs from the Canyon de Chelly illustrate and typify the kind of prehistoric ritual that might have occurred at Lascaux and in much of the Mediterranean some 30,000 years ago. Painted hands, or nega-tive imprints of the hand, are

*Canyon de Chelly,
superimposed hand
prints, wounded man,
zigzag, Anasazi Indians,
circa 1300*

*Temple of Seti I,
Abydos, XIX Dynasty,
1318–1304 BC (note
the entasis and Gouda
bases)*

30,000 years ago. Painted hands, or negative imprints of the hand, are characteristically superimposed on or near sacred icons. Often a dance with singing, clapping and rhythmical music accompanied a ceremony which might concern the hunt. A shaman, dying animal and zigzag pattern are often depicted. With many different cultures the differences in meaning for each of these rites are as significant as the universal symbolism, but the generic nature of this activity is still important. From contemporary hunting and gathering cultures we may infer that the rituals had an ecstatic component, both aided by and free from drugs. Rapture and trance could be induced as much by rhythmical dancing and mental concentration as they can be today.

Under the Egyptian dynasties cosmic ritual is given a mythic and rational component. Shamans become priests, but the role of mediating between everyday reality and natural forces remains a primary goal. Half-animal, half-human figures also remain as symbols of this mediation. Today at Abydos, which has roots in one of the oldest shrines, the feeling of such ancient rituals is very much present. A dark, polychromatic ambience is occasionally broken up by shafts of intense sunlight. On the walls and columns the formulae recited during the daily performance are recorded at length in the Temple of Seti I (XIX Dynasty).

Images of the pharaoh ordering the seasons, restoring nature, con-

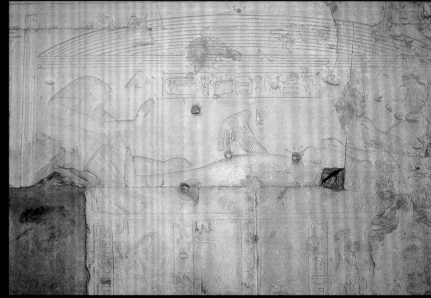

When slain Osiris was hidden in the four-tiered Djed-Column, before he was reborn, Abydos

Horus, son of Osiris, the protector of the pharoah, gestures in benediction at the feet of the dead king wearing the white crown of Upper Egypt, Abydos

agricultural strife such as that between Cain and Abel) is reborn again each spring. The corn god is symbolised by the magic Djed Column, sign of agricultural regeneration and the annual flooding of the Nile that literally renews nature. The phallic shape of a column with a four-tiered echinus at the top – representing branches of the tamarisk tree – is often surmounted by the sun. Osiris, after being slain by Seth, was hidden in this tamarisk-column when his sister/wife, Isis, was searching for him, in order to make him whole. There are some natural metaphors here all centring on potency: the connection of death and rebirth, hiding and rediscovery, and the annual cycle of corn growth and Nile flood. The mystery of the way nature renews itself is here the basis for religion and art.

Many other proto-Christian symbols are present with Osiris and Isis, but the sexual nature of rebirth is more explicit at the temple of Abydos than in a church. In one side chapel of the temple, funerary and sexual rites are clearly combined. The dead king is equated with Osiris and is shown with an erect penis (subsequently chipped away by those seeking to partake of its magical potency). Above it flutters a hawk, transformation of Isis according to experts, while at the foot of the pharaoh-Osiris is the result of this regenerative act, the son, Horus, the falcon and traditional protector of the pharaoh. He raises one hand in benediction while touching the knee of his father with the other. The gesture

Bundled papyrus columns, Luxor, Amenhotep III, 1400–1362 BC

of hands at either end of this sexual/ funerary act gives it a very human tenderness, and the overall mood of the temple still works to evoke a profound sense of regeneration. Even today women use parts of this temple for fertility rites.

Much more abstract in its ritualistic role is the primary place of the huge column. It is given a sensuous, steady, rhythmical beat. Indeed, Egyptian architecture is essentially trabeated – based on the column and beam – and, when one walks through it, all the details march to an hypnotic drum beat set by the columns. At Thebes and Luxor one progresses past rows of sphinxes or rams or pylons as if following a military march. The repetitive rhythms are as stately and moving as anything the Greeks and Christians achieved, with the same architectural idea, thousands of years later.

It may be hard to imagine that such ceremonies could be sensual or even enjoyable, but when one looks at the delicacy of the papyrus columns – and their beautiful intercolumniations – it becomes possible. When one sees the kind of barque carried in the procession, and the way nude bodies, decorated architecture, plants and animals are equated, the idea becomes even plausible. The Litanies of the Sun specify the acclamations with which the Sun-God Re was greeted, when at eventide his barque reached the entrance to the nether world. Twelve hours of darkness, night, sleep – death – were seen as a prelude to morning, rebirth and life. Egyptian architecture is an ecstatic celebration of this metaphor.

Temple of Hatshepsut, Deir el-Bahri, XVIII Dynasty, 1490–1469 BC

Alabaster barque and baldachino with stylised lotus columns, rams, and nude figures, Tutankhamun, XVIII Dynasty, 1333–1323 BC, Cairo Museum

BODY IN ARCHITECTURE

We read our bodily states into nature, a truth lampooned in the eighteenth century as the 'Pathetic Fallacy'. Pathetic or not, we have continued to commit this fallacy for the very good reason that there are deep analogies between body and nature and, more significantly, that we relate to living and dead things through empathetic projection. The body in sculpture and architecture is an eternal theme, but one that has waxed and waned over 30,000 years. Its importance for architecture varies from depicting historical events (the theme of the caryatids) to being a system of proportions and harmony, to being a form of sexual and religious identification.

Most ecstatic of all is the projection of bodily states and moods on to building. Architecture viewed in this light is muscle and tissue, svelte outline and modelled breast, voluptuous limbs rounded by shadow. Architects have always exploited this sensuality. The Greeks articulated Doric columns with thin fillets that catch the light; Le Corbusier once defined architecture as 'the masterly, correct and magnificent play of volumes seen in light'. It is the metaphor of the body which lies behind this preoccupation with light sculpted building.

The oversized body was first used by the Egyptians as a symbol of sensuous potency. Figures of Akhenaton, sometimes called 'the first individual in history' because he introduced Monotheism and a very personal, elongated style into art, are noticeably hermaphroditic. His feminine face, big lips and swelling hips are as striking as the

Akhenaton ('pious to Aton'), XVIII Dynasty, Cairo Museum

Colossi of Rameses II and, smaller, wives and servants, Abu Simbel, XIX Dynasty, 1304–1237 BC

Sun God Helios, Colossus of Rhodes, from Fischer von Erlach, Entwurf einer historischen Architektur, 1721

Mount Athos turned into Alexander the Great by the architect Dinocrates, from Fischer von Erlach's treatise

proposed 'Ecstacity' as a logical extension of the metaphor spread around the whole, pulsating metropolis.

The problem with Dinocrates' proposal, aside from the obvious faults, is that anthropomorphism on this scale is not empathetic but alienating. Perhaps the most effective use of the device is when it is suggestive and half merged with other meanings. The artist Francesco Primaticcio achieves this in a French grotto. Here rustication, another sign of nature in its rough state, and the body are given equal weight with other symbols of ecstatic pleasure, such as Pan.

The body became such an omnipresent canon in the Renaissance that columns, whole churches and even their details were proportioned in its image. So well established was this argument that it could be used to criticise shapes considered awkward or inhuman. Thus, when Bernini proposed for St Peter's in Rome the metaphor of 'welcoming arms to embrace the pilgrim', this very argument could be turned against him: when a body image was superimposed on the colonnade design, it resulted in the grotesque distortions of twisted claws. QED.

Michelangelo's equation of the body with the sculptural modelling of mouldings remained a standard for the Classical language of architecture well into the twentieth century. Many French and English architects followed his example of sculpting pediments, keystone and mouldings in counterpoint with the light and shadow cast by human

F Primaticcio, Grotte des Pins, Fontainebleau, 1540s

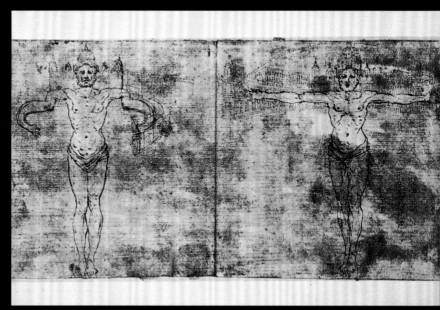

Criticism of Bernini's plans for Piazza of St Peter's, Rome, by the Unknown Critic, c. 1657 (after Wittkower)

figures. This 'Architecture of Humanism', as Geoffrey Scott described it, really does engage the mind's eye: we project our balance, structure and physical states on to modelled surfaces. We identify with inanimate matter and the environment is humanised as a metaphor of life.

In an industrial landscape, where the metaphor of the machine and its neutrality dominate, this sensuality becomes all the more valued and it is no surprise that many Post-Modernists have adopted anthropomorphism as one part of their attack on dead form. The body image is most effective, as with Primaticcio's work, when it is veiled and tied into functional necessities. Yet, as Nigel Coates is showing with the hermaphroditic figures under London's Millennium Dome, our culture is still fascinated by the explicit colossi, especially those that can be entered and explored.

A Beresford Pite, 82 Mortimer Street, London, 1896

Bearded Gorgon, ante-fix from Campania, 55 BC, Getty Museum

The bearded gorgon from a Greek antefix typifies so many of these contradictory icons. It laughs like a comic book character and sticks out its tongue between twisted teeth. In the gardens of Bomarzo several stylised monster heads, used as shelters, swallow the visitor. Count Orsini took the conventional signs of bulging eyes and flaring nostrils to symbolise Hades eating its sinners. Federigo Zuccaro applied the same idea to his palazzo in Rome, but with the unlikely result that the monster of hell swallows not an evildoer but a window.

Federigo Zuccaro,
Palazzo Via Gregoriana,
Rome, c.1592

Architects under
Francesco Caratti,
Cernin Palace, Prague,
1718–20

At the Cernin Palace a relative of this beast chokes on a gag, at the Villa D'Este water pours from one of its three mouths. The smiling and scowling face changes the mood in a garden and church, while the face to make-up the face can be encountered in a bathroom. They may not all induce ecstasy, but they do work to set the temper of a place.

Villa D'Este fountain with stone eagle, fleur de lis and grotesque head, Rome, c.1685

Lucas von Hildebrant, Upper Belvedere, sphinx, Vienna, c.1722

The Face House has a long history both in canonic and popular architecture. Palladio uses the analogy and an eighteenth century Hebrew text, which Carl Jung cites, characterises the archetype. The furnace and kitchen are bowels and stomach, the turrets are ears and the doors and windows are mouth and eyes. Anthropomorphic metaphors remain the principal alternative to mechanistic ones, and surprisingly Eric Owen Moss has crossed these alternatives in the portrait of an owner. He looks out through heavy metal struts under his hat to welcome the approaching visitor.

Charles Jencks, Bathroom Face and Ear Face, Santa Monica, 1982

Eric Owen Moss, Owner's Face, Culver City Office, 1996

It is interesting to trace an architectural idea as it follows a trajectory across time. The dome is one of the oldest and most solid shapes and goes back to the concrete bath houses of the Romans from the first century BC (false, corbelled domes have an even longer pedigree). The dome inevitably follows compressive stresses and visually it is invariably heavy. Thus the move to dissolve the dome is an attempt to make it lose weight, float in space, defy gravity. Ecstasy is typified by such motives – anti-gravity, out-of-body experience – and thus the dissolving dome is one of its chief tropes.

Octagonal dome with cross arched ribs, Cordoba c.961

The first move starts with several experiments at Cordoba in the tenth century. Arched ribs intersect across a square and on the two diagonals leaving an octagonal configuration. The voids between are ornamented, suggesting that they could be windows, and visually the dome starts to spin. Guarino Guarini developed this idea in several churches actually admitting indirect light through the overlapping arches. Baroque and Rococo architects furthered the dissolution of the surface and made the metaphor of floating more explicit – angels support the surface – while I have pushed the same idea in another direction of illusion using layered tiers and a corkscrew mirror to symbolise infinity.

Antonio Gherardi,
Avila Chapel, Santa
Maria in Trastevere,
Rome, 1680

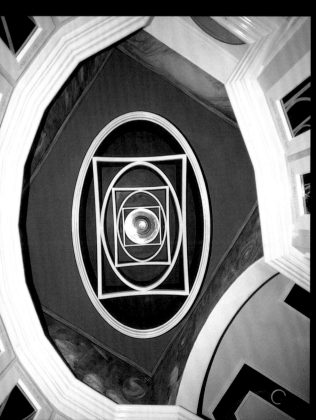

Charles Jencks,
Cosmic Oval Dome,
London, 1983

Paolo Portoghesi, for a mosque in Rome, combines both layered horizontals and intersecting ribs to make the dome float; its only drawback is that, at the centre, more light is not allowed to dissolve it even further.

The most interesting experiments with fracturing the dome today are being carried out by Eric Owen Moss in Culver City, Los Angeles. Several of these are so smashed about and dissolved that one is hard put to call them domes, but they all have a fascinating way of breaking up light and reaching for the stars. Moss has discovered that by stacking many different architectural elements in layers, against the sky, they pull the eye very strongly through space as it tries to read the different cues of depth. Here is the architectural equivalent of ecstatic lift-off.

*Paolo Portoghesi,
mosque, Rome,
1990–97*

*Monta Mozuna,
Kushiro City Museum,
layered dome, 1982–84*

With the Rococo, architecture becomes a backdrop for the personification of moods, the Passion of Christ and the setting for total theatre. Above all it is a backdrop for gratifying the senses, for affairs of the heart, for display of personal affection. Every detail, colour, line and sculpture is brought together into the *Gesamtkunstwerk*. The interior conceived as a total work of art has many precedents, but it never before reached such frenzies of integration, even in minor building types such as the Summer Pavilion at Amalienburg. The usual function for this outburst of rhetorical skill is religious and the usual place for its culmination is the high altar.

The Asam brothers, for a tight, thin, urban church in Munich, produced a triple explosion at this point: cross and starburst, St John and sunburst, then at the top Christ in passion. His red blood is taken up, metaphorically, in the undulating lines of stucco lustro which lead the eye towards him. Spiral Solomonic columns frame the scene both like a proscenium arch and baldachino. As with Ecstatic Architecture in general, genres and boundaries are crossed, different types are melded into each other. The whole effect is heightened by viscous surfaces, sparkling gilt and back-lighting.

Egid Quirin Asam,
St John Nepomuk,
Munich, 1733–46

At Rohr, top, back and side-lighting accentuate the figure ascending in religious ecstasy, though her dress and expression are more that of Lady Bountiful strewing flowers than of Mary meeting God. The ability to sustain a convincing work of total art is often undercut by the inability of so many different artists and craftsmen to keep to the same message. Sentimentality, rather than sentiment, results when too many artisans are asked to be ecstatic on demand. Nevertheless, the number of successful examples in southern Germany is impressive.

Asam brothers, Rohr Church high altar, 1722–23

At Die Wies church, Steinhausen,
Dominikus Zimmerman uses overlapping ovals to keep the eye
moving continuously in shallow
layered space. In the main 'nave'
light bounces around the white
arcades, while in the chancel the
forms turn blue and then red to
focus the mind on Christ's Passion.
He is shown under a small baldachino, suffering under the yoke of
the Cross, and bleeding.

Dominikus Zimmerman,
Die Wies Church,
Steinhausen, 1746–54

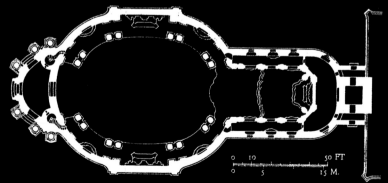

Much Rococo, however, suffuses and dissolves a space with reflected light. Rocaille details make it shimmer; ghost pilasters layered on top of each other make it dance in vertical stripes. At Vierzehnheiligen the architect seems to make light glow out of the walls and explode the space, as if one were inside the usual sunburst. The ever-present baldachino now occupies a central space and seems to writhe upwards in foam, as if it were an ocean wave bursting with enthusiasm through the floor. Rocaille drips and splatters appreciatively in release – can heaven really be this orgasmic?

Michael Thumb,
Obermarchtal
Cathedral, 1686–92

Balthasar Neumann,
Vierzehnheiligen
interior, 1774, altar
by Kuchel, 1762

Art Nouveau was manifested under many aliases: Jugendstil, that is Youth Style, Modernismo, Metro Style, Noodle Style, Yachting Style, Liberty Style, Whiplash Style and so on, through each metaphor of otherness. The root metaphor is located somewhere between free-dom, discovery and transcendence, as if one were going on a holiday from everyday life into the unknown. The best Art Nouveau, that of Antoni Gaudí, understands this motive of the search, for going beyond. It is a very romantic impulse which, at its most sublime, reinvents culture as a cosmic process, as an eruption of volup-tuous nature right in the dirty heart of the industrial city.

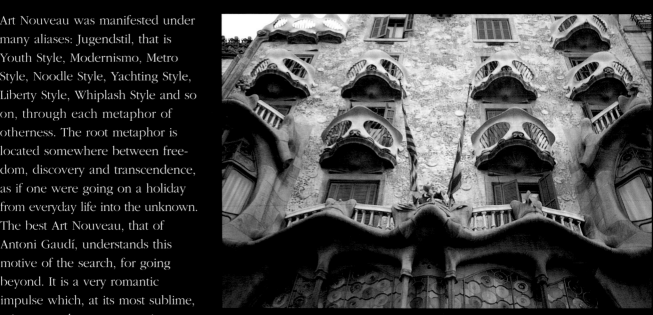

Antoni Gaudí, Casa Batló, Barcelona, 1905–7

Antoni Gaudí, Casa Milà, Barcelona, 1905–10

Gaudí, the sophisticated primitive, understood this more than anyone else: one of his few surviving cryptic insights was: 'originality is going back to origins'. Indeed, he reinvents European culture. In his hands ordinary mass-produced material is turned into images of the Mediterranean – seaweed and the kelp that washes to and fro on the surface of the sea. This forms that backdrop to the Casa Batló, interspersed with the bones and death masks of those Catalans murdered by the Madrid power structure (Francoists, understanding this, burned his drawings and smashed his models).

Architectural metaphor is deeper and richer with Gaudí than with any architect who has ever lived. His Casa Milà is a profound and profoundly mixed metaphor about the relations between Catholic religion, nature and city life. Again, nature in the form of undulating water creatures – not only seaweed but jellyfish – becomes a major theme, but it is played off against counter-themes – the 'quarry' of rustic stone and ecstatic faith (crosses which whirl up on the rooftops like multibladed, Christian helicopters). Only Puritans remain unmoved by the inventiveness and conviction with which this is carried through – and there have been quite a few of them in recent Anglo-Saxon architecture.

Antoni Gaudí, Casa Milà, Barcelona, 1905–10

Gaudí's work in the Parc Güell, which had a utopian programme to establish a new form of city living, is the most naturalistic. Undulating seats are formed to the human bottom, back and arm positions, while columns, with notched cells and splayed capitals, take up the language of the surrounding palm bark and fronds.

Hector Guimard, also a structural rationalist, took his ideas from the observation of growing plants. His various designs for the Paris Métro transformed this, the most mechanistic instrument of city life, into green, wavy tendrils and drooping flower-buds. Entrance balustrades also make use of a motif we have seen before, the grotesque face, although here it is, ambiguously, also transformed into a beetle and a bat.

Antoni Gaudi, Parc
Güell, Barcelona,

Hector Guimard, Paris
Métro, 1901

When the Metro Style reached Belgium, Victor Horta commented, 'grasp the stem, leave the flower' – do not be taken in by prettiness, go for the underlying structure. Thus his best work has the calligraphic quality of thin plant stalks waving in the wind and one finds such images from nature in both expensive private houses and socialist meeting halls. They suggest a more voluptuous way of life than conventional city living.

An extraordinary idea underlies the project of Art Nouveau, the notion that everything hard could be transformed into the equivalent of an orchidaceous climber. Soft City before it was named. Other Belgium designers, such as Gustav Strauven, developed natural imagery, including Horta's whiplash metaphor, and refined it to a delicate high art. In Art Nouveau, from Helsinki to Chicago to Barcelona, one finds the great alternative to the triumph of the mechanistic metaphor, the hope that one could live in a second nature that was sensual and everchanging.

Victor Horta, Horta house and atelier, Brussels, 1898–1900

Gustav Strauven, entrance gate, Brussels, c.1901

Frank Lloyd Wright exploited geometry and mass-produced ornament in the same way as the Egyptians to create repetitive rhythms which have an hypnotic effect. His Barnsdall House, commissioned by an oil baroness who wished to build an avant-garde theatre complex right in the heart of movieland – Los Angeles – typifies his mixture of large geometric solids studded with endless, stylised figures.

In some senses, as we will see, the building is a portrait of its extravagant owner. The ornament is fascinating, if excessive. It marches over the background surface, as it does in Egyptian architecture, to a relentless beat. Solid and void, shadow-line and blank surface, building and planting, stucco and stylised hollyhock – these are the primary contrasts which are played in extreme opposition. Indeed, the handling of the contrasts is the architecture.

Frank Lloyd Wright, Aline Barnsdall Hollyhock House, Los Angeles, 1917–21. The 'Mayan' sitting room

flower. As a result, nature and construction are given equal weight and threaded through each other like a three-dimensional tapestry. Even though the architecture is repetitive, it is never boring because each plane is broken, every flat surface displays one of four types of ornamental hollyhock.

In terms of rhetoric we are in familiar territory. This is the *Gesamtkunstwerk* with every detail subordinated to a highly redundant whole. Overpowering unity, forceful Beethovian rhythms, no dissenting lines, no 'complexity and contradiction'. This 'organic architecture' is also called a 'Californian Romanza' by Wright, because it is such a powerful image of white rectangles gliding over a green hill. The layout is axial, not only Egyptian but Beaux-Arts Classical, with endless streamlined pathways shooting out to offer views over Los Angeles.

Indian women at key points

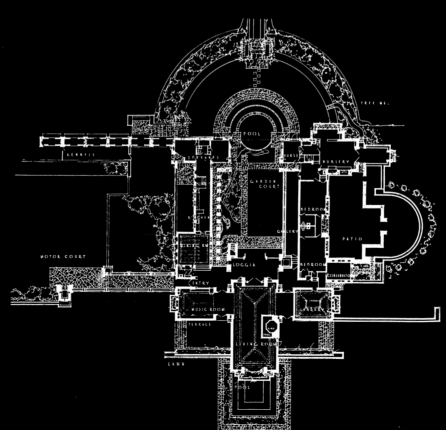

Plan of Hollyhock House, 1920

The hollyhock flower is stylised in four ways: at important transition points as the figure of a sitting Indian woman; as sentinels which guard the roof and run along as column capitals; as a dental frieze of squat figures; and, in the dining room, as tall-back dining chairs – the most flower-like. Counterposed to these heavy shapes are the delicate lines of the leaded windows which have an asymmetrical rhythm.

All this ornament culminates, as it often does with Wright, around the hearth. Here light spills from a translucent latticework (air) over the fireplace (fire) surrounded by a mini-moat (water), while straight ahead is the heavy masonry centre-piece (earth). What do these four elements focus on? Aline Barnsdall herself? I don't know, but this 'rest-less spirit', as Wright called her, was always running around America in her car, getting away from it all, and one can read the stylised holly-hock here as the restless spirit on the move, zooming ahead in her open-air dragster. Fanciful perhaps, but then the whole building and programme has a fanciful air. It is close to being pure architecture about itself, an excessive concentration on the architectural sign, and this is what pushes it into the realm of Ecstatic Architecture.

Asymmetrical leaded windows in symmetrical piers

Hearth with the four elements

Ekstasis:
Dematerialism and Movement
Paolo Portoghesi

The word *ekstasis*, common to all the main European languages, stems from the Greek εκστασισ, meaning shift and deviation, but also agitation, disturbance, delirium. Within Catholic theology the word designates the utmost degree of mystical experience, when the soul is ravished in contemplation. Religious *ekstasis* can often cause supernatural visions and levitation can take place. In secular terms *ekstasis* can signify a state of intense delight, which takes one away from reality; a particularly violent form of ecstatic rapture, which can occur when enjoying art or an enthralling performance, like a rock concert or the feats of a footballer. In architecture the adjective 'ecstatic' can reasonably designate a quality that transports the beholder away from reality to a supernatural domain.

Baroque Ekstasis

To clarify the meaning and potential of the term, it is helpful to analyse a case in which representation of *ekstasis* was the goal of an artist, in a work where the languages of sculpture, painting and architecture are all used. A good example is the Cornaro Chapel in Santa Maria della Vittoria in Rome, built by Gian Lorenzo Bernini from 1645 to 1654. The statue of the saint is placed in a cylindrical space of elliptical plan, an aedicule overlooking the altar, lit from the top through a little window almost invisible from below, like the spotlight used in theatre to highlight the protagonist. A theatrical logic informs the whole architectural, sculptural and pictorial complex: the aedicule acts as a traditional stage, since in two little side choirs some members of the Cornaro family appear, like spectators at an event which splits into two simultaneous actions. As well as the saint's *ekstasis*, which takes place on the earth, the Cornaro, from their privileged vantagepoint, can see another scene painted on the chapel's barrel vault, one which is set in heaven. The painted scene is like a chasm oriented towards the

Gian Lorenzo Bernini, The Ecstasy of St Teresa *and Side Choir, Cornaro Chapel, Santa Maria della Vittoria, Rome, 1645–54*

Gian Lorenzo Bernini, Cornaro Chapel, elevation
and detail of altarpiece

celestial infinite instead of downwards. Bernini's representation of St Teresa was literally inspired by the saint's own account of her experience of *ekstasis*: 'I was seeing an angel next to me, in corporal pose . . . I could see he had a long golden dart in his hands. It seemed to me that he wounded my heart by it, reaching for the viscera.'

With respect to this account Bernini acted as a musician who interpreted an opera's libretto, translating into image the accurate description. The angel is realistically represented in the act of piercing through the saint's heart with the golden arrow, and the saint appears exhausted, uttering the invocation, 'Jesus, the sweetness is too much, either be less gentle or widen my heart'.

Bernini used at least three devices to communicate effectively the condition of *ekstasis*, and in all of them sculpture and architecture are closely connected.

The first strategy is that of clearly visualising 'levitation', a phenomenon with no explanation according to physical laws, which takes place when a person in mystical rapture rises and floats in the air for some time. Cases of levitation are reported in the hagiographies of such famous ascetics and visionaries as Francisco d'Assisi, Ignazio di Loyola, Filippo Neri, Maria Maddalena de' Pazzi, Giuseppe da Copertino but the most evident accounts are those reported in the autobiography of Saint Teresa of Avila. The term rapture, used by Teresa, expresses very well her sensation of being overpowered by a force impossible to resist, one that carries the body upwards against gravity. Bernini managed perfectly well to convey the impression of levitation by placing the statue of the saint on a little cloud that seems to float in the air.

Bernini's second device relates to the lighting and it is more subtle. Light comes through a hidden window on to a stained glass, flooding on to the saint and the angel. Light materialises itself in a bundle of light beams created by its passage through slats of gilded wood.

The third and more architectural strategy concerns the aedicule which houses the sculptural group. The starting point of the design is the Classical aedicule in the Pantheon, but the model is developed into an oval-plan space, a kind of little chapel decorated with pilasters and 'crowned' by a coffered cupola with its lantern. It is a tight space opposed – because of its 'unreality' – to the real one, where the beholder belongs. It can be characterised as 'sacred space', since there everything takes place at once. The contrast between this space, where the saint was caught in rapture, and the real and secular one, is accentuated by the theophany of the fresco on the barrel vault.

Sacred time is, according to the definition of Mircea Eliade, 'the time reversible by nature', indefinitely recoverable and indefinitely repeatable. It is an ontological time *par excellence*, as Parmenides insisted, always identical to itself and one which neither changes nor runs out. That Bernini's scheme for the Raimondi Chapel included the representation of sacred time is confirmed by the altarpiece depicting the Last Supper. The Catholic Mass, in fact, represents the repetition in real time of an historic event which, since it happened in a sacred time, can be not only recalled, but also repeated through transubstantiation – the conversion of bread and wine into the body and blood of Christ when consecrated in the Eucharist.

It might be relevant to notice, as has Robert T Petersson, the way Richard Crashaw, a poet of that time, dedicated to Saint Teresa something similar to the Raimondi Chapel, likewise aiming at the full involvement of the visual, musical and conceptual aspects of the depicted phenomenal.

Petersson writes, 'Crashaw shows ecstasy flowing into eternity without any interruption of space and time, without any diminuition in brilliance'. He compares the two creators, the sculptor and the poet:

yet Bernini and Crashaw present the event completely without violence. For both the significance of the wounding is internal. It is the effect of the event on Teresa which is primary. Although Crashaw's lines keep the Saint at a respectful distance, they have the authentic intensity of her autobiographical account of the dart penetrating deeply, much sweetness caused by this intense pain 'so sharp that it made me utter several

moans, so excessive was the sweetness caused by this intense pain that one can never wish to lose it'. The paramount characteristic of this 'death' is its utter gentleness.

As in the sculptural representation of the saint, most of the transfiguring effect is due to an abstract element which is not descriptive, it is like the virtuoso treatment of the mantle with its endless folds. In Crashaw's text it is the conceptual and sound play that conveys to the reader the secret meaning of the event, and this culminates in the middle of the poem, where the Saint is in direct communication with Christ:

> **Sweet, not so fast! Lo thy fair spouse**
> **Whom thou seekst with so swift vows**
> **Calls thee back, and bids thee come**
> **T'embrace a milder martyrdom.**
> **Blest pow'rs forbid thy tender life**
> **Should bleed upon a barb'rous knife;**
> **Or some base hand have pow'r to race**
> **Thy breast's chaste cabinet, and uncase**
> **A soul kept there so sweet. O no,**
> **Wise heav'n will never have it so.**
> **Thou art love's victim and must die**
> **A death more mystical and high.**
> **Into love's arms thou shalt let fall**
> **A still surviving funeral.**
> **His is the dart must make the death**
> **Whose stroke shall taste thy hallowed breath;**
> **A dart thrice dipped in that rich flame**
> **Which writes thy spouse's radiant name**
> **Upon the roof of heav'n, where aye**
> **It shines, and with a sovreign ray**
> **Beats bright upon the burning faces**
> **Of souls which in that name's sweet graces**
> **Find everlasting smiles. So rare,**
> **so spiritual, pure and fair**
> **Must be th'immortal instrument**
> **Upon whose choice point shall be sent**
> **A life so loved. And that there be**

Fit executioners for thee,
The fair'st and first born sons of fire,
Blest seraphim, shall leave their choir
And turn love's soldiers upon thee
To exercise their archery.

It has been assumed that Richard Crashaw actually saw the Raimondi Chapel and fell under its spell, but this hypothesis does not hold. The more probable reason, then, must be the *zeitgeist*, the spirit of the times, Crashaw and Bernini belonging to a common cultural climate, in this particular case Catholic Europe. And in fact, Crashaw, although he was born in England, remained, by courageous and difficult choice, a Catholic.

The spirit of the times, which far from being a divisive factor often brings opponents closer and helps reconcile rivals, also assists in explaining some analogies and differences between Bernini's work and the church of San Carlo alle Quattro Fontane in Rome, designed by Francesco Borromini in 1634. Here the only artistic language used is that of architecture aided by decoration employed as an iconological factor. The result gains in intellectual intensity what it loses in sensuality, because it captures a different mystical temperature, one that is more medieval and less Baroque. This is often called a 'Borrominian Baroque', defining its Northern manifestation, as opposed to the 'Berninian Baroque', which is more Mediterranean and solar.

The *ekstasis* of Borromini's architecture stems from his desire to enable the beholder to contemplate specific aspects of the Divine. Fra Juan de San Bonaventura, who supervised the construction of the church, relates this intention. Fra Juan writes in vernacular Italian: Everyone says what the Queen of Saba said to King Salomon when the two met.

Id est: Verum est sermo quem audivi in terra mea super sermonibus tuis et super sapientia tua: et non credeba narrantibus, donde ipsa veni et vidi oculis meis et probavi, quod media pars mihi nunciata non fuerit: maior est sapientia et opera tua quam rumor quem audivi. **[True is the tale I was told in my homeland about your sermon and your wisdom: but I didn't believe the tellers, hence I came myself and I saw with my own eyes lest a great part was not told to me and I made sure that broader is your knowledge and work than the rumours that I've heard] . . . Everyday we see people from all**

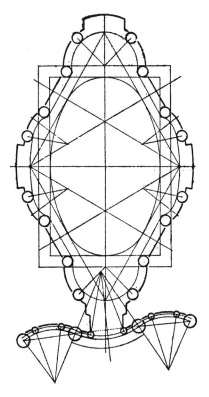

Francesco Borromini, San Carlo alle Quattro Fontane, Rome, 1634–82, view of ceiling and plan

Francesco Borromini, San Carlo alle Quattro Fontane, Rome, section

countries – Germany, Flandres, France, Spain, Italy and even India – who have heard about the beauty, vagueness, and architecture of this church, coming to see it, and when they find themselves in the church, they go on and on looking up and around, because all things in it are set in a way that one refers to the other, and from the gallery we see those people looking around without uttering a word, and they cannot resolve to leave for a while, and most admirable is that the more they have seen, the more they wish to see, and the same people come back many times. Why would they return? Because the church has got in itself something of the Divine.

Do you recall St. Peter's words about the Blessed Angels? St. Thomas and others say that those Angels long for the Holy Spirit: but this is deceiving: how can the Angels long for the sight of the Holy Spirit if they are Blessed and therefore they always see and rejoice? Beda answers: 'All things in the world, before seeing them one longs to see them, and after having seen them they become so annoying that one no longer wishes for them. But the Divine Essence gives the beholder so much delight that though it fills the soul with sweetness not only one is never fed up with it but he wishes for more.'

As with Bernini's chapel, we can identify the methods used by Borromini in order to attain the effects described by Fra Juan. The first consists in relating all the plastic forms, and the architectural order in particular, to the light source which is placed very high. The second consists in contracting and dilating the space, so that when one moves about in the church the space gives the sensation of attending to a living, breathing being. The third consists in an amazing synthesis of regularity and irregularity, both responding to the spatial parameters of the Classical tradition, which they upset in pursuit of dynamic equilibrium.

The lighting device is exemplary: the overhang of the moulding is as shallow as possible, to avoid casting shade on to the parts below. The decoration, which according to the critics of the time was the weak point of Borromini's architecture because it betrayed a *horror vacui*, makes every surface contribute to the luminous polyphony of the whole. The quality of skimming light recalls Leonardo da Vinci's chiaroscuro and it refers to the religious interpretation of light as the beginning of cosmogony.

Paolo Portoghesi, the Mosque of Rome, 1975–95

The contraction and dilation of space is the proper architectural means used to achieve the ecstatic quality of the image. In a subtle way, Borromini proposes a synthesis of two opposed systems: the two apses on the main axis, and the two on the shorter axis. Modern topology provides us with the theoretical instrument anticipated by Borromini, highlighting the prophetical implication of his thought.

The affinity between his combinatorial operation and religious ecstasy is that both transport one away from reality. The static space of experience is contracted and dilated in a way which prefigures possibilities typical of our times with the spread of computers and experiments of virtual reality.

The theme of levitation, considered as the physical display of *ekstasis*, finds an analogy when one passes from the side chapels to those in the apse, and the proportions change from Renaissance to 'Gothic'.

The dualities – vertical–horizontal, Classical–Gothic, dilated–compressed – provide a clue to the most provocative expedient: it consists in the synthesis of rule and exception, regular and irregular, traditional and innovative. The design of San Carlino's architectural order stems from a cornice belonging perhaps to the Temple of the Sun on the Quirinale Hill, not far from the site of the Borrominian church. Starting from the Classical model, the architect translates it into another language to solve the problem of making the light 'dance', which produces a soft passage of chiaroscuro.

Arata Isozaki summarises an important point in relation to the Church of San Carlo:

Looking back on the Baroque period at the large number of Baroque works we cannot deny that Borromini's work is highly personal, and it does not belong to a universal system as much as the readily assimilable work of Bernini's, such as S. Andrea. Consequently Borromini's work has not been consumed, it still remains fresh and not able to be borrowed. From this example we may infer that to establish a manner which rejects systematization is to choose a destiny of continually struggling against the epoch. Borromini's choice of this direction is the reason why his work has produced such an immutable effect. We may say that Borromini's S. Carlo alle Quattro Fontane is the supreme example of such a goal.

Paolo Portoghesi, the Mosque of Rome

PROPHETIC EKSTASIS

The artistic cult of *ekstasis* does not end with Baroque, it returns in cycles. An ecstatic aspect can be ascribed to Etienne-Louis Boullée's architectural images. In his design for the Newton Mausoleum the beholder is placed in absolute centrality before the sky, hence removing all bonds to the earth. And starting with Boullée – and even Beethoven – the whole modern adventure is dotted with ecstatic objects, the purpose of which is to take one away from ordinary experience so as to grasp the 'future'

A champion of *ekstasis* was, by all musical means possible, Alexander Scriabin (1872–1915). His goal, like Bernini's, is to operate simultaneously with time and space. His most celebrated musical composition, *The Poem of Ecstasy*, illustrates a state of the soul where a man-god through love and sex, creativity and procreation, completely frees himself from all bonds. He writes in a notebook,

The soul must long for absolute being, for ecstasy. How is ecstasy possible? Ecstasy is the apex of activity. Ecstasy is the peak. Protest and the wish for a new order lie in the present state of things. In the form of thought, ecstasy is supreme synthesis. In the form of feeling, ecstasy is supreme beatitude. In form of space ecstasy is the supreme development and destruction. I cannot consciously experience anything if at the same time I do not have an unconscious experience of all the rest. The unconscious side of my work takes part in everything. The Universe is an unconscious process of my creativity. Man is my individual conscience in objective form.

After the Russian Revolution a prophetic value was ascribed to his work.

In the twentieth century, and post-Scriabin, the theme of *ekstasis* undergoes a long eclipse. In architecture it reappears with Bruno Taut's Expressionistic drawings and in some works by Alvar Aalto, such as the church in Imatra, and those of his followers Jørn Utzon and Reima Pietilä. Much architecture in the 1980s and 1990s, has chosen to transport us away from the real world to an oneiric one, and create a rarefied atmosphere. Within this architecture, which tends to oppose the virtual to the real, producing agitation, disturbance and delirium, it is important to distinguish between the buildings which have chosen to mime catastrophy, explosion and earthquake, and those where the aim of dismantling and violence

Paolo Portoghesi, Church of Sacra Famiglia, Salerno, 1968–74

pursued by Deconstruction, invites in its place the goal of proper *ekstasis*, which cannot be separated from delight and reconciliation. It seems to me that the most interesting aspect of those attempts lies in founding the new ecstatic condition on contemplation, in a search for a unity which implies a new alliance between man and nature.

NATURE AND EKSTASIS

In my own work I have often aimed to arouse in the beholder an ecstatic condition, especially with the church of Sacra Famiglia in Salerno (1968–74), the Mosque of Rome (1975–1995) and a hall of the Montecatini spa (1987). With the Mosque of Rome I elaborated a strategy based on the evocation of sacred time and space, through a lighting technique which dematerialises matter. 'Levitation' is rendered in a very explicit way through the relationship between the columns and the roof, which consists of two structures: the one transparent and light constituted by the intertwined arches, and the other heavy and homogeneous constituted by the 'telescopic' domes. The telescopic device implies an ascending motion. Light, in fact, comes from the top, through the dome's slits, and from the bottom, through a horizontal window along the whole enclosing wall, resulting in a diffuse lighting. A similar device was attempted in the church of Sacra Famiglia in Salerno, whose vault consists of four concentric cylindric windings, three of them representing the Holy Trinity, and the fourth representing the overall unity, double in size to signify that unity predominates over multiplicity.

An 'ecstatic research' has also been carried out in the hall of the Montecatini spa, although here the inspiration is not religion but the myth of Gaia – the Earth as a living organism – an idea introduced by James Lovelock's book *Gaia* (1979). The search for ecstatic space does not address the supernatural here, as it does in the mosque or the Salerno church, but the 'natural', informing the beholder with a perception beyond the realistic image of the structure of the trees, similar to the process of abstraction pursued by Mondrian in the series of paintings dedicated to the theme of the tree.

According to Wright's *In the Cause of Architecture* (1908):

A sense of the organic is indispensable to an architect . . . where can he develop it so surely as in this school? A knowledge of the relations of form and function lies at the root of his practice; where else can he find the pertinent object lessons Nature so

Paolo Portoghesi, Montecatini Spa, 1987

readily furnishes? Where can he study the differentiations of form that go to determine character as he can study them in the trees? Where can that sense of inevitableness characteristic of a work of art be quickened as it may be by intercourse with Nature in this sense? Japanese art knows this school more intimately than that of any people. In common use in their language there are many words like the word 'edaburi' which, translated as near as may be, means the formative arrangement of the branches of a tree. We have no such word in English, we are not yet sufficiently civilized to think in such terms, but the architect must not only learn to think in such terms but he must learn in this school to fashion his vocabulary for himself and furnish it in a comprehensive way with useful words as significant as this one.

The ecstatic component of the Montecatini's structure lies, after the manner of Borromini, in the vertical dilation, and in the opposition of the plain design of the floor, a simple combination of black and white tiles, to the organicity of the branched columns. The idea of an 'awakening' of forms in the flood of light refers to Portland's phanerogamic studies on the phenomenon of the flower's 'self-presentation': 'The reason for the endless vegetable forms is not the conservation of species but the self-presentation, appearance to light'. Recently a new horizon has opened up, where *ekstasis* relates to a 'Neo-Modern' return to the *tabula rasa*, exemplified by the works of the masters of Deconstruction; in particular, that of Frank Gehry, in relation to whom it may be appropriate to talk of an 'ecstasy of dismembering'. But is it possible to combine *ekstasis* and violence, ecstasy and a virtual conflict? These seem to counterbalance the pacifism, if not the peace, of our times.

I believe *ekstasis* and violence are irreconcilable. Although *ekstasis* is an abnormal state of consciousness, a release from reality, it still implies a process of contemplation; hence it is a disturbance that leads one to a state of well-being and contemplative joy. Nor should one forget the religious origin of the term, which does not suit the individualistic delirium of the artist who wishes only to express his own personality. Instead of Gehry, whose design is informed with playfulness, even 'mockery', it is best to ascribe ecstatic quality to the work of architects such as Nigel Coates, Ron Arad, Shin Takamatsu, Alessandro Mendini and Philippe Starck, but also Imre Macovecz, in addition to personalities like Reima Pietilä and Jørn Utzon.

Ecstasy
Neil Leach

Gian Lorenzo Bernini, The Ecstasy of St Teresa,
c.1650

It is ironic that one of the best known works of any architect of the Baroque is not a building but a sculpture. Gian Lorenzo Bernini's exquisite sculpture, *The Ecstasy of St Teresa*, in the Cornaro Chapel of the church of Santa Maria della Vittoria in Rome has captured the interest not only of enthusiasts of the Baroque, but also of contemporary theorists from the world of psychoanalysis and literary criticism. Why, then, has this piece proved of such interest to these theorists, and how might their thoughts on this sculpture begin to inform a discussion of contemporary architecture?

THE RAPTURES OF ST TERESA

St Teresa of Avila (1515–1582), a Carmelite nun and religious mystic, was a reformer who established her own order, and set up seventeen new convents throughout Spain. Regarded as a saint in her lifetime, she was renowned for her ecstatic religious experiences, which Bernini knew well. Certainly, her 'visions' had been cited on her canonisation at Rome in 1622, within thirty years of when Bernini began his sculpture.

To the contemporary world she is most famous for her vivid, auto-biographical accounts of her ecstasies or 'raptures':

. . . Rapture is, as a rule, irresistible. Before you can be warned by a thought or help yourself in any way, it comes as a quick and violent shock; you see and feel this cloud or this powerful eagle rising and bearing you up on its wings.[1]

The eagle is, of course, God. And a fundamental aspect of the rapture is the sensation of being raised aloft by God:

One sees one's body being lifted from the ground; and though the spirit draws it up after itself, and does so most gently if one does not resist, one does not lose consciousness. At least I myself was sufficiently aware to realize that I was being lifted.

1   Saint Teresa, *The Life of Saint Teresa of Avila*,
    trans. J M Cohen, Penguin (London), 1957, p136

The majesty of One who can do this is so manifest that one's hair stands on end, and a great fear comes over one of offending so great a God.[2]

2 Ibid.

Overwhelmed in this state of religious convulsion the rapture takes hold. It is a bitter-sweet moment of ecstasy that is both pleasurable and painful. In this her ecstasies share something of the sublime:

One seems to be on the point of death; only the agony carries with it so great a joy that I do not know of any proper comparison. It is a harsh yet sweet martyrdom. . . .[3]

3 Ibid, pp140–41

As the word 'ecstasy' implies, this experience takes place beyond the body. *Ekstasis* means a 'standing outside' of the body. The ecstatic rapture is an experience of the soul, an extra-corporeal sensation. During the process the eyes remain closed or half-closed, but, in any case, the individual is almost oblivious to the outside world:[4]

4 'The eyes are generally closed, although we may not wish to close them, and if occasionally they remain open, the soul . . . does not perceive anything or pay attention to what it sees'. Ibid, p143

. . . Generally the senses are disturbed; and though absolutely powerless to perform any outward action, the subject still sees and hears things, though only dimly, as if from far away. I do not say that he can see and hear when the rapture is at its height; and by 'its height' I mean those times when the faculties are lost, because closely united with God.[5]

5 Ibid, p142

But what does begin to emerge is a markedly erotic undertone to St Teresa's description of her raptures. In particular, when she is being stabbed with 'a long golden spear', as in the sculpture by Bernini, her language shares much of the discourse of erotic pleasure:

In his hands I saw a long golden spear, and at the iron tip there appeared to be a point of fire. This he plunged into my heart several times so that it penetrated to my entrails. When he pulled it out, I felt that he took them out with it, and left me

utterly consumed by the great love of God. The pain was so severe that it made me utter several moans. The sweetness caused by this intense pain is so extreme that one cannot possibly wish it to cease, nor is one's soul then content with anything but God. This is not a physical, but a spiritual pain, though the body has some share in it – even a considerable share. So gentle is this wooing which takes place between God and the soul that if anyone thinks that I am lying, I pray God, in His goodness, to grant him some experience of it.[6]

It is through her raptures, then, that St Teresa comes into union with God. In this state of ecstasy, the boundary between the self and the 'other' is broken down. The ecstasy allows a form of mystical 'bonding' which, while religious, shares certain characteristics with a more carnal form of love.

THE EROTICS OF ECSTASY

It is this connection between mysticism and the erotic that intrigued the French writer and critic, Georges Bataille (1897–1962). Bataille was a theorist who delighted in the excess, a critic who both wrote and theorised on the subject of obscenity and eroticism. Alongside his own often highly obscene fictional work, *The Story of the Eye*, he wrote a theoretical text, *Eroticism*.[7] In *Eroticism* Bataille examines the way in which the religious always threatens to fold into the erotic. He compares and contrasts these two overlapping moments, and while he is not interested in simplistic equations which collapse the two into the same category, reducing the religious to the erotic and treating rapture as little more than a form of sexual orgasm, he admits that there are 'staggering similarities and even corresponding or interchangeable characteristics in the two systems'.[8]

Eroticism was published in 1957, within a few years of Bataille's death, and it is perhaps no coincidence that a key theme in this text is that of death and its relationship to life in the context of the erotic. For it is not simply that on occasions the propagation of life may lead literally to death, as in the case of a mother dying during childbirth. Rather, the two become entwined within the erotic moment. At an explicit level there is a direct connection between death and the erotic in the French slang for orgasm, *'le petit mort'* – 'the little death'. Bataille pursues this theme through the figure of St Teresa who acknowledged the sense of death that accompanied the

6   Ibid, p210

7   Georges Bataille, *The Story of the Eye* by Lord Auch (1928), trans. Joachim Neugroschal, Penguin (Harmondsworth), 1982; *Eroticism* (1957), trans. Mary Dalwood, Marion Boyars (London and New York), 1987

8   Marie Bonaparte compares this rapture directly with the sexual act, citing the example of a nun who had experienced such raptures, only to discover in later life when she left the convent and married, that these 'raptures' had been in fact a form of sexual orgasm. St Bonaventure also notes that mystics are not infrequently 'sullied with the flow of carnal flux' during their ecstasies. Georges Bataille, *Eroticism*, pp24–26, 247

vital experience of her raptures. For Bataille it is as though the desire to live 'to the limits of the possible and the impossible with ever-increasing intensity' brings with it the desire for death, but it is a desire that amounts – paradoxically – to a transcendence of death:

It is the desire to live while ceasing to live, or to die without ceasing to live, the desire of an extreme state that St Teresa has perhaps been the only one to depict strongly enough in words. 'I die because I cannot die.' But the death of not dying is precisely not death; it is the ultimate stage of life; if I die because I cannot die it is on condition that I live on; because of the death I feel though still alive, and still live on. St Teresa's being reeled but did not actually die, because of her desire actually to experience the sensation. She lost her footing, but all she did was to live more violently, so violently that she could say that she was on the threshold of dying, but such a death as tried her to the utmost though it did not make her cease to live.[9]

9 Ibid, pp239–40

Thus, for Bataille, the erotic and the mystical come together in the ecstatic moment, and they do so within the symbolic framework of life and death.

The French psychoanalyst, Jacques Lacan (1901–81), was also fascinated by Bernini's sculpture, *The Ecstasy of St Teresa*, and an image of it is used on the front cover of his volume, *Encore*.[10] In this work Lacan focuses on the sense of *jouissance*, a term that has been used in English literature since the sixteenth century and might literally be translated as 'pleasure', referring to the 'pleasure' of the text. In French *jouissance* maintains a certain erotic purchase that has been lost in English appropriations – it has a more overtly sexual connotation, referring to the pleasure of the sexual act itself.[11] If Post-Structuralist writers from Derrida to Cixous constantly evoke the term, it is in this extended sense of the 'erotic' pleasure to be derived from reading the text.

10 Jacques Lacan, *Le Séminaire de Jacques Lacan*, Libre XX, '*Encore*', Éditions du Seuil (Paris), 1975, p70

11 In French the verb '*jouir*' is slang for 'to come'

In Lacan the term *jouissance* exceeds the simple sense of 'pleasure', but it presents a problem. *Jouissance* comes to be perceived as unbearable suffering, although at an unconscious level it is experienced as a form of pleasure. It is the moment of *jouissance* that reveals a trace of the intensity of the 'real', which – in Lacanian terms – is always inaccessible. The 'real' cannot be symbolised. It remains a foreclosed element that may be approached, but never grasped. Hence the bitter-sweet ecstasies of St Teresa offer a perfect example of *jouissance* at work. When we encounter an object that bears witness to the 'real', like the 'terrifying' angels of Rilke's second 'Duino Elegy', it is always a traumatic event.

ARCHITECTURE–RELIGION–LOVE

How, then, might we appraise Bernini's sculpture from an architectural point of view and what insights might it offer for an ecstatic engagement with architecture? What begins to emerge is a sense in which the erotic shares similarities with the state of religious ecstasy, as observed by Bataille, and the *jouissance* of the text observed by Lacan and others. If we include architecture and other objects of aesthetic contemplation within the latter category of the 'text' we might begin to recognise that the mechanisms in play with aesthetic contemplation replicate those in both an erotic and a religious encounter. Hence we might explore the fundamental nature of aesthetic contemplation by comparing it with these latter two. Throughout, there is a sense in which the engagement with the 'other' – in the case of architecture, the built environment – amounts to a forging of a relationship with the 'other'. It is here that psychoanalysis offers an insight in the way we relate to architectural space. It has generally been assumed that human beings *do* identify with the built environment – how else, for example, might we ground any discourse which relies on the principle of identification, such as critical regionalism, except on these premises? But the precise mechanism has not been explored. I wish to suggest a symbolic one, which can be understood through psychoanalysis, the great unwritten chapter of twentieth-century architectural theory. We symbolically identify with the 'other' when we come to 'situate' ourselves in the built environment.

Such an approach might begin to address certain as yet unanswered questions in architecture. How is it that we progressively 'grow into' certain architectural environments, for example, after a few days we eventually feel 'at home' in an alien hotel room? How can a once alien and hostile element be 'appropriated' as part of our familiar world view? For example, satellite dishes no longer seem so out of place in our contemporary streets. Without giving a detailed analysis of the mechanism employed, some answer can be found in the notion of symbolic appropriation. Over time we symbolically appropriate the unfamiliar such that it begins to constitute our horizon of consciousness. Symptomatic of this is the very temporal nature of the way in which we 'grow into' and adapt to our environment in an almost chameleon-like fashion, so that with time we eventually feel 'at home' in it. It is within this framework that concepts which have a deep symbolic purchase, such as that of 'home', can be understood. The very fluidity and transferability of the concept of 'home', which may shift with time from one place to another, reveal it as a term of mere symbolic identification, which is forged over time by the ego itself.

This appropriation is, of course, no more than a mythic appropriation. It is as though the basic mechanism that underpins religious identification with the 'other' – the mythic leap of faith – can be found in all identifications with the 'other'. This might be extended to include the identification implicit in love, and also aesthetic identification. Religious affiliation, emotional bonding and aesthetic appreciation can therefore be seen to share the same inherent structure. All these forms of identification must be based on some belief system which 'claims' a link between the self and the other at the level of the symbolic. For, according to psychoanalytic theory, even in the case of love there is no *actual* link between the self and the other. '*Il n'y a pas de rapport sexuel*' – 'there can be no sexual relationship' – as Lacan has observed. Love therefore becomes a 'mirage that fills out the void' of the impossibility of a relationship between the two sexes.[12] To those involved, of course, love appears as decidedly real. But, significantly, within Lacanian theory what we take for the real is not the 'real' itself, but an appearance. This is not to reduce love merely to some realm of fantasy. While love depends upon the existence of an image, true love, as Renata Salecl observes, always aims at the kernel of the Lacanian 'real', that raw element whose trace appears in *jouissance*.[13]

This same principle holds true for religious devotion where 'faith' fills that gap between the self and the 'other' – between the worshipper and God. For 'faith' is a mythic construct. There is nothing to authorise the supposed communication between the worshipper and the Divine except 'belief' itself. The worshipper simply 'believes' that he or she is in communication with God. Faith, like love, takes the form of a 'mirage', and while, like love, it is not 'real', it appears so to the worshipper.

The principle would likewise hold true for an aesthetic identification with anything, such as the built environment, where a symbolic attachment

12 Renata Salecl, *New Formations*, No 23, Summer 1994, pv; see also Salecl, 'Love: Providence or Despair', in ibid, pp13-24

13 Ibid, pv

comes into play. Here we must speak not of physical engagements – the actual presence of an individual in an environment, but of the symbolic attachment which gives that presence its meaning. 'Attachments', in this sense, are no more than symbolic attachments, susceptible to shifts and erasures, as the full fluid dynamic of unconscious identification comes into operation. The world around us should be understood as fundamentally 'other'. We may forge symbolic links with that environment – identify with it – but this can only be understood as a symbolic identification that shares the essential characteristics of love and devotion. The mechanism by which we begin to feel 'at home' in a building is similar to the mechanism by which we fall in love and develop religious faith.

The psychoanalytic theorist, Julia Kristeva (1941–) has explored how a constructive engagement with art and architecture entails an openness to the 'other', and embodies an essentially 'erotic' dimension. She lays great emphasis on the process of making art, which must remain an essentially 'amateur' activity in both senses of the word: as 'non-professional' and as 'loving'. For Kristeva, professionalism detracts from art, while artists come to express their 'love' through the process of making art:

In the ideal hypothesis, the artist succeeds in probabilizing, in relativizing, his own production, as though it were a living system that lives only on condition of being open to the other.[14]

A central theme here for Kristeva is that of 'agape' (Gr αγαπη), a form of higher love which enacts a union with God. *Agape* is more mystical than mere 'eros' (Gr ερωσ), the common form of love. It is a selfless, charitable love. *Agape* is not desire. Love as *agape* in Kristeva's work, as John Lechte has observed, 'is the basis of a dynamic potential in the process of identification.'[15] Art, for Kristeva, plays a similar role to love. From a psychoanalytic perspective they both serve to broaden horizons and maintain psychic space: 'The amorous and artistic experiences, as two independent aspects of the identificatory process, are our only way of preserving our psychic space as a "living system", that is, open to the other, capable of adaptation and change.'[16] Art, therefore, has the potential to open up a series of 'relationships' with the 'other'. It allows one to identify with the 'other', always a plural identification. It is in this process of identification that the erotic and vital dimension of art is revealed. To be closed off to the potential of art amounts to a form of death. An encounter with art is an encounter

14 Julia Kristeva, quoted in John Lechte, *Julia Kristeva*, Routledge (London), 1990, p215

15 Lechte in ibid, p216

16 Julia Kristeva, quoted in ibid, p215

with difference that holds the potential to forge new relationships in a world where 'to live' means 'to love'. And art, like love, may play a form of substitute role for religion. As Lechte observes:

> **To refuse difference here, to be closed off to the dynamic aspect of identity, is also to begin to die – certainly in a symbolic sense, and probably in a physical sense as well. Without God . . . the speaking being in postmodern times risks becoming a stunted version of humanity. Love . . . can compensate for God, and so can art, in Kristeva's view.**[17]

17 Ibid, p 216

Kristeva's work links art, love and religion, as does that of Bataille and Lacan. Moreover, Kristeva situates her discussion of art within the specific framework of life and death.

THE PARADISE OF ECSTASY

A fundamental aspect of this symbolic identification is the notion of 'sacrifice' that underpins an ecstatic engagement with the 'other', such as we find in the ecstasies of St Teresa. While 'sacrifice' is more usually understood within a religious context, its essential mechanism might also be found in other domains, such as love and art which are likewise centred around themes of 'life' and 'death'.

In Freudian terms we might understand aesthetic contemplation as related to the death instinct. Freud's late theory is centred around the conflict between *eros* and *thanatos*, between love and death, between life instincts and death instincts. *Eros*, as the life instinct, serves to counter the tendency towards *thanatos*, the death instinct, and acts as a force to complicate life. It continually counteracts and delays the death instinct. *Eros* is therefore set in opposition to *thanatos*, that which seeks resolution and quiet. In Freud, the death instinct can be seen to emanate from the moment of birth itself. Birth is seen as a violent trauma which upsets the pleasure of the time in the womb. Yet the memory of this period in the womb remains, and subsequent life is governed by a desire to regain this lost quietude, this lost paradise. Life is dominated by a regressive compulsion, a desire to return to the womb. This striving for 'integral gratification' dominates all subsequent life. Thus, for Freud, the drive towards equilibrium that results is none other than a 'continuous descent toward death', where death finally provides that longed for resolution and quiet.

Composition often involves a 'harmonic' resolution of tension. In contemplation of aesthetic composition we might recognise a moment that replicates the mechanism of the death instinct. We become 'one' with that composition, as we give ourselves over to it in aesthetic contemplation. The harmonic resolution of tensions within the aesthetic composition may serve to resolve the tensions within the viewer. Great art mediates. But the mechanism here is equally related to the life instinct, in that there is also a vital experience that comes out of aesthetic contemplation. It is not perhaps, as Marcuse supposes, that the split between the death and life instincts is resolved as they come back together in aesthetic contemplation. Rather they can be seen to operate in tandem. In engaging with the work of art we become one with the work of art – we succumb to the death instinct – in order to live on *through* the work, by being invigorated with the life instinct. In other words the process leads to a revitalisation through the work of art. Aesthetic contemplation becomes a way of transcending death at a symbolic level.

As an example consider Narcissus gazing into a pool to contemplate his own beauty. He sinks into the pool and drowns, and as a result, a flower, the narcissus, starts to grow beside the pool. The death instinct is realised, but it serves only to feed the life instinct. Narcissus dies in order to give life to something else. This process is replicated in all forms of aesthetic contemplation. A similar mechanism is employed in religious devotion. Christ 'dies' on the cross in order to give life to others. The mechanism is that of the 'sacrifice', and it is one that applies to aesthetic contemplation, erotic encounters and religious devotion alike. We surrender ourselves to the 'other' in order to live on through the 'other'. We give ourselves up to death in order to transcend death.

Just as in a religious context the sacrifice of the religious moment opens up the possibility of living in some paradisiacal realm, so we might recognise the condition of love, and equally the state of being at one with one's aesthetic environment, as having an essential paradisiacal component. Through the 'bliss', the ecstasy of being at one with the environment, one lives on in a state of almost religious intoxication, a paradise of the senses. Nor is it coincidental that in the Renaissance it was the emblem of paradise as an original state of unity and connectedness that prompted architects and artists to attempt to recreate a heavenly paradise on earth. For it was not simply through the symbols themselves – the four rivers of paradise represented in Renaissance gardens, and so on – but through a symbolic identification with the beautiful that they sought to replicate this paradise.

ECSTASY IN ARCHITECTURE

What, then, is the consequence of all this for architecture? First is the social role. We might counter the argument made by those who take a position critical of the 'Society of the Spectacle', and consider the reign of the image in contemporary culture as a source of alienation. According to such an argument, individuals can only understand themselves through the image, and are thereby alienated from their true selves. Against this we might claim that the image – and, by extension, any form of design, including architecture – is potentially a source of identification, not alienation. A crucial factor, of course, must be the quality of the design. In the context of architecture it is not enough to say that *any* design may provide us with that source of identification. Clearly, the human psyche has the capacity to adapt to almost any surroundings, to the point that one might grow attached to even the most uninviting of spaces. But the important point is that *good* design will surely facilitate that process. In such a case it will not be necessary for the ego to expend effort in symbolically forging a link with what is fundamentally alien or unpleasant. The ego will naturally feel at home in a pleasant environment, assuming that it has developed a sense of aesthetic appreciation.[18]

In order for architecture to have this role it must conform to the sensibilities of the age. Here we might reflect upon claims by Omar Calabrese and others that we live in the 'Neo-Baroque' period.[19] It is an age of fractals, rhizomes, displacements, folding, warping and cloning; it is an age of theatricality and excess which challenges the limiting strictures of rationality that governed our previous Modernist paradigm. While our language of forms does not correspond exactly to the language of the Baroque, there is a clear parallel set up in the way it challenges the ortho-doxy of Modernism, just as the Baroque challenged the orthodoxy of the Renaissance.

We might recognise in these forms a certain ecstatic spirit that shares something of the erotic dynamism of Bernini's sculpture of St Teresa.

18 Someone, for example, with little sense of aesthetic awareness, but a heightened sense of acoustic awareness, might feel 'at home' listening to certain musical works, and may have little concern for the aesthetic quality of the built environment

19 Omar Calabrese, *The Neo-Baroque*, trans. Charles Lambert, Princeton University Press (Princeton), 1992. Calabrese gives the chapters of his book headings such as 'Rhythm and Repetition', 'Limit and Excess', 'Detail and Fragment', 'Instability and Metamorphosis', 'Disorder and Chaos', 'Complexity and Dissipation' and 'Distortion and Perversion'

Perhaps, then, while the forms break free of Modernism, with a licence characteristic of the Baroque, the sensibility of the age might be more properly described as the 'ecstatic'. It is an age, after all, in which we are constantly being bombarded with sublime, intoxicating imagery. It is an age in which the nightclub, with its strobe lighting and pulsating music, has become the temple to a new religion for the younger generation. It is, above all, an age in which the use of certain kinds of narcotics, such as the drug Ecstasy, offers a form of paradisiacal release.

It is precisely the drug Ecstasy that offers us some insight into our contemporary sensibilities, a drug that has always been linked to paradise, as suggested by its original name. As Nicholas Saunders observes, 'Ecstasy was first used by Americans as an aid to psychotherapy and personal development. They regarded it as a sacrament which could allow them to be their true, uncorrupted selves in the state that God created mankind before the Fall, and they named it "Adam" for that reason.'[20] It is a drug, moreover, whose effects bear remarkable similarities to the raptures of the ecstasy of St Teresa – it reportedly allows one to 'stand out' from the self, the ill and the diseased to 'step out' from the body. It therefore replicates the *ekstasis* experienced by St Teresa. It has, so it is claimed, a certain 'uplifting spiritual quality'. In other words, it not only enhances a sense of religious communion, but it also has the effect of raising one up as though on a cloud, or on the 'powerful eagle' which St Teresa describes that bears one up 'on its wings'. Indeed, it has been used for precisely this purpose as an aid to prayer by members of religious communities. A Benedictine monk, Brother Bartholemew testifies, 'When used appropriately it is almost sacramental. It has the capacity to put one on the right path to divine union with the emphasis on love, vertical love in the sense of ascending.'[21]

To claim that a popular drug might aid religious devotion is one thing; to claim that it has similar characteristics to religious devotion is another. Such a claim might appear somewhat irreverent. According to Lacanian theory, however, ecstasy is a form of *jouissance*, and the key question in all modes of ecstatic enjoyment is how one 'anchors' one's *jouissance*. For Lacan, as Slavoj Zizek observes, there is a 'separation' between 'the hard kernel of *jouissance* and the ways in which this kernel is caught in different ideological fields – *jouissance* is "undecidable", "free-floating".'[22] Hence there is little fundamental difference between what

20 Nicholas Saunders, *Ecstasy Reconsidered*, Nicholas Saunders (London), 1997, p6

21 Ibid, p191

22 Slavoj Zizek, *The Plague of Fantasies*, Verso (London), 1997, p50

St Teresa experiences and what may be experienced in contemporary night clubs: 'The enthusiasm of fans for their favourite rock star and the religious trance of a devout Catholic in the presence of the Pope are libidinally the same phenomenon; they differ only in the different symbolic network which supports them.'[23] As Sergei Eisenstein observed, referring to the work of St Ignatius of Loyola, the positive figure of God only comes second after the moment of 'objectless' ecstasy.[24] In other words, while ecstasy itself is ahistorical and not associated with any particular territory, it must be 'located' somewhere, fixed by concentration of psychic energy on to some object of desire.

Discourse surrounding the use of the drug Ecstasy notes that one of its effects is to produce a feeling of empathy towards the world, a feeling of oneness with other people. What is essentially an aesthetic experience takes on a social dimension. Far from being a purely indulgent gesture – a narcissistic withdrawal from the world – the taking of Ecstasy induces an almost religious sense of empathy towards the environment and fellow human beings. A similar effect can be fostered by ecstatic architecture. Such an architecture allows one to feel at one with the world, to forge a mythic sense of identification with one's surroundings.

But what exactly might an architecture of ecstasy look like? Some clue, no doubt, might be found in Bernini's exquisite statue, *The Ecstasy of St Teresa*. It would be an architecture with the capacity to reflect the ecstasy which Bernini so convincingly conveys, an architecture that responds to a certain contemporary sensibility. This is not to say that ecstasy can be the 'property' of specific architectural forms; rather, ecstasy is a condition of consciousness by which we engage with those forms. Nonetheless, particular forms respond to particular sensibilities, and certain forms therefore 'lend' themselves to promoting a condition of ecstasy.

Hence we might recognise in the work of Nigel Coates, Greg Lynn, Zaha Hadid and Ron Arad an architecture with the capacity to reflect an ecstatic spirit, an architecture that helps to lift one on to a higher plane, and to induce a sense of bliss; an eroticism of architecture; an intuitive sense of free form that breaks down the potential alienation of the unduly rational language of Modernism; an architecture of the senses; an architecture which invigorates and which also has the potential to foster a sense of spiritual oneness with the world – an architecture of ecstasy.

23 Ibid.

24 Sergei Eisenstein cited in ibid

Ecstatic Space
The Royal Academy of Arts Debate

Robert Maxwell

Ecstasy, as distinct from art – and there are many kinds of art and many kinds of sensation in art – is to do with a certain excess which actually affects you in your body.

Robert Maxwell

Robert Maxwell I would like to make a distinction between architecture as art and architecture as ecstasy. We have lived through – and when I say lived through, I am talking literally, from the twenties through to the nineties – a century when architecture was released by the new century into abstraction; all of art was released into abstraction. Only architecture chose to put into that abstraction the dogma of function. So we have lived for eighty years under the dogma of function. No architect will stand up and say that he's not doing the functional thing. Finally, at the end of this century, we see architects standing up and saying, 'What I am doing is art' – point one. Why did it take so long for architects to be more courageous? – point two. Ecstasy, as distinct from art – and there are many kinds of art and many kinds of sensation in art – is to do with a certain excess which actually affects you in your body. I have to say that I was extremely affected by Paolo Portoghesi's description of Borromini's San Carlo alle Quattro Fontane in Rome, pointing out that in its oval disposition, it was, as it were, breathing: first the long and then the short. He could have communicated the extraordinary way that the breathing is articulated, is brought together, by the cornice which runs through the whole church at the head of the order. . . . It has no breaks; it is entirely modern; it is entirely horizontal. It is the most superb piece of sensational architecture in the world. And so what I would like to say here involves two things: architecture as an art, and secondly, what are the categories of art – of which ecstatic art is certainly one?

Jane Harrison I think that the architecture/art debate is a dead one. Raising the issue about function does not mean that the only other thing that architecture can be is art, and I think that one of the things that is interesting about this debate is what was alluded to at the beginning of Nigel's talk, to do with trying to cope with extreme conditions of excess,

Nigel Coates

which is a reality. There is a whole range of uncharted territory that I think people are really beginning to grapple with now, and it's not about simply trying to represent a condition.

Nigel Coates I find the word 'art' very difficult. As an architect I think that the work of most architects who execute drawings is occasionally looked at, and people say, 'Oh, but it's art!' . . . That is dangerous in a sense, because if the agenda that you're bringing to architecture includes aspects of well-being and a sense of intimacy, belonging, reflection, amplified sensation and perception, all those things are close to the agenda of art, but it is not the same site.

Sally McErith I am quite interested in the words that are around tonight, the two words ecstasy and sensation in particular. I think even the word sensation is very much a Radio 1, low-brow, tabloid sort of word, and I think that it was interesting with regard to Paolo's talk that the immediate connotations of the word ecstasy were churches and religion. If you asked most people under twenty-five what were the first five things that come to mind when you mention the word sensation, religion would probably be quite low down the list. It is very sad, but I think more people find more religious sensation in a Calvin Klein shop on Bond Street than they do in all these wonderful churches.

Charles Jencks This relation to commerce was raised by Nigel: he said that ecstasy is now common in our culture.

Nigel Coates I was trying to lead into a discussion about the relationship between contemporary lifestyle and all its multiplicitous aspects of desire, and what sort of architecture would go with that. I wasn't dismissing the religious part of it, simply saying that the sites have shifted into a much more convoluted contemporary condition.

Frans Haks I think what you see in architecture, as Nigel has shown, is that the publicity value is enormous; it is more important than the function. Therefore, you could say that if the publicity value is enormous – and it should be very specific in form, then the function can be what you want.

Matthew Hardy You are talking about architecture that exists only as an advertisement. This week I received my first postcard of the new Bilbao museum, and my friends had written on the back, 'There's nothing much else in this town'. I think that building is working to attract people to visit it . . . Going now to the idea of religion in the past, I think this specifically and very consciously used light, music and smell to control sensation, to create a sense of ecstasy. All these things, we recognise, are now borrowed by cinematography, by commercial interiors. Very early on in the discussion I was contemplating the idea that the historical interiors we saw were of solid surfaces visible under light, as Le Corbusier might have described them, whereas the most recent examples we saw were all reflective or transparent. I wonder if what was historically an ecstatic architecture of hyper-visibility, if you like, has now transmogrified itself into a modern concept of a kind of ethereality of architecture.

Paolo Portoghesi

I don't think that it is possible to translate ecstasy through violence. Ecstasy can be translated in sweetness and laughter but not in violence.

Paolo Portoghesi

I wonder if what was historically an ecstatic architecture of hyper-visibility, if you like, has now transmogrified itself into a modern concept of a kind of ethereality of architecture.

Matthew Hardy

Paolo Portoghesi I want to pose some questions, because I have seen the *Sensation* exhibition, which is solely an exhibition of violence, typical of end-of-the-century France. In my opinion, architecture is not only art; architecture must resolve some problems. In each epoch, it has solved problems – of power, of survival – practical questions. The escalation of violence does not aid us in solving problems, especially at the moment . . . I don't think that it is possible to translate ecstasy through violence. Ecstasy can be translated in sweetness and laughter but not in violence.

Kenneth Powell Following on from that point, the concurrence of our symposium with the exhibition is interesting but highly controversial, and in a way pure chance, because I don't see much in common with the works of the architects who have presented this evening and all those present such as Ron, Nigel, Jan, Richard, who are all radical architects. But I think the element that is consistent in their work is a sort of humanism. The Jewish Museum, by Libeskind, is the opposite end of the spectrum from this exhibition. It is pro-humanity. It's also architecture not only in the newest sense but also in the most traditional. The Baroque masters who designed those churches in Rome would have understood that building, warmed to it, responded to its spatial qualities and what it communicated . . . I feel that our scrapping of the functionalist tradition is fine, but let's not scrap the humanistic tradition in the Modern Movement at the same time.

Neil Leach I do see a huge connection between the *Sensation* exhibition and the question of ecstasy; they are very close to each other. Without going into great detail, it strikes me that the key thing about this exhibition is that it is shocking; it's deeply shocking. We know from Walter Benjamin and Charles Baudelaire, who speak about shock as the essence of Modernity, that shock has an intoxicating effect, that basically shock anaesthetises. We've spoken about alcohol, intoxication, in connection with ecstasy. I really don't have a problem with that. I think there is a close affinity, particularly between the works in the exhibition and what is going on here.

Jane Harrison In response to the exhibition, my sense of it was that it was much more to do with rhetoric than it was with violence, and that, if anything, the exhibition presents the pitfalls of attempts at producing spectacle. It falls into the trap that if you are not being shocked by it, you're bored by it. This, in a way, connects to some points that were made earlier about the validation of a building being the five minutes of ecstatic experience. The other side of the coin is how do you talk about the experience the second time, the third time, the fourth time, once the initial impact of the spectacle has worn off . . .

Robert Maxwell There is a real problem here, the problem of our society which aims to be democratic. Democracy, the Greek word, originally meant the rule of the mob. What everybody can instantly understand and respond to is mediated by rhetoric. It is ready-prefabricated and pre-

Kenneth Powell

I do see a huge connection between the *Sensation* exhibition and the question of ecstasy, it strikes me that the key thing about this exhibition is that it is shocking; it's deeply shocking, and shock has an intoxicating effect, basically shock anaesthetises.

Neil Leach

digested so that everybody will get the point, whereas all the high emotions of art are only possible through cultivation. We have the problem of the elite and the popular. What is immediately ecstatic is what is rhetorically projected as ecstatic. This is not going to last; this is going to be last year's thing.

Adrian Weston There's another interesting point that has been buried in this. Listening to what Paolo was saying about religious ecstasy, we have a profound juxtaposition between a historical construction of ecstasy, where the same ecstatic point was revisited daily, weekly, the twelve points of the cross, the repeated, the ritualised, and a situation and a society which is based on not revisiting the same ecstatic moments. You might be looking for a similar trip to last time, but by a different route. I think that also ties into what was said before about transparency in buildings and differences in textures, and I think this whole issue of transience relating to the ecstatic moment is quite central to that.

One of the interesting aspects to this discussion on ecstasy is how is it possible to work as an architect, and to sustain within an architectural project, a condition which doesn't either produce a kind of numbness or a kind of instant moment.

Jane Harrison

Jeremy Melvin The first thing I want to say is that there is a long tradition of architecture trying to make sense, to build rhetoric, to make a construction that comes literally and metaphorically out of violence. Any form of Christian architecture is, on one level, an attempt to deal with one of the most mind-boggling acts of violence – if one accepts Christianity – that one can possibly imagine. The same could be said, in a contemporary context, of Libeskind's Holocaust Museum. In a sense, the Holocaust Museum is the first great monument that is trying to come to terms with the incredible act of violence which has scarred our century.

Neil Leach I wish to suggest that the statue of St Teresa, which has been the subject of so much discussion today, is emblematic of the potential role that architecture has in today's society: architecture should be something that people relate to, identify with, in a particular way. In Bernini's statue of St Teresa, which has been spoken about by Bataille and Lacan, is a moment of erotic and religious ecstasy. What happens when you surrender yourself to the other is precisely what I would say should be happening in an architectural moment. One should be surrendering oneself to the other, engaging with an architectural environment.

Richard MacCormac This mode of ecstatic architecture is very specific. I am not demeaning the opportunity, and it is an interesting discussion. The location in space and time for ecstatic architecture is rather particular. On the other hand, I wonder what is and is not ecstatic. When Fermat's Last Theorem was declared a few years ago, all the mathematicians were ecstatic. Is that ecstasy? Are intellectual achievements ecstatic?

Kenneth Powell I think that is the point that unites literature, music, science, art. You are talking about a moment of creativity, and a perception of creativity by other people.

Richard MacCormac . . . And the outcome of intellectual creativity. What is important to me about the work of Borromini is that it is ecstatic, but the intellectual underwriting of the experience is also ecstatic, because it is so absolutely extraordinary. Think of doing that without computers!

Kenneth Powell Isn't the ecstasy in architecture when something is new. The greatest ecstasy must have been between the wars, when you think of it. If you were a modern architect in England in 1930, what was the ecstasy like then? You were actually striving against the mass to really create something worthwhile – fighting for it.

Charles Jencks The question I think we have to return to at least once in the evening: is there or is there not a useful phrase 'ecstatic space – architecture', or 'euphoric space – architecture', or is it simply a fall-out of consumerism, a much broader cultural situation? . . . I think this is an architecture of persuasion. We have the Church, desperate to convert people in the post-Reformation period, building these kind of sensuous ethereal buildings. We have Ron Arad with his planning application in Hampstead, desperate to convince the authorities to allow it to be built. We have the Cartier Centre; what is that if it is not an attempt to persuade people to buy Cartier? We have lurking in the background this fluctuating relationship of architecture and commerciality, which is nothing if it's not persuasion.

Frans Haks If you talk about ecstatic architecture and you realise that religion has lost its importance it is imperative to look at the most important

Richard MacCormac

The new ecstatic architectures will be biotechnical, cybernetic, fleeting and be much concerned with facilitating information flow.

Neil Spiller

commissioners of potential, real ecstatic architecture. I am talking about Disneyland, about the Guggenheim. If you don't talk about that, or say it's of lesser value, you're missing the point.

Charles Jencks Frans brings up this point: it's either museums trying to rejuvenate provincial cities like Bilbao, which has been tried in Britain and in America, and worked to a certain extent; or it's international corporate elites, who come out of fantasyland but are no longer fantastic. They want to use ecstasy – if that's the right word – as a tool to get their market share. No one disagrees; those are two real forces. That's a description of what's happening.

... the ecstatic is the moment where the new becomes visible.

Robert Maxwell

Robert Maxwell But this means that ecstasy is never the same. It always has to be resought at the point where things are just becoming visible in the general march of time, in the general march of culture. There was a time when the only way you could give in to sexual aspirations in public was by bending down in front of St Teresa in a church. That was the point at which erotic possibilities emerged. But nowadays erotic possibilities don't come out much in church; they come out in other places. There's always a new site where this thing comes. What you're getting close to saying, Charles, is that the ecstatic is the moment where the new becomes visible.

Nigel Coates I don't think it is just a question of the ecstatic function shifting from religion. It's also the fact that the ecstatic component coincides with the fields of communication that invade all of our lives. Therefore, whereas religion was a separate thing that in some way offset the banality of your daily toil in the fields, there is an aspect of the pervasiveness of information technology which in some way invades your body, and your body and your mind must respond to it. That's why ecstasy is in some way part of our civilised condition now. It is not just a transfer from religion to beauty or aesthetics. It is not that distant; it's intimate.

Charles Jencks Can I raise the point that both Frans Haks and Nigel Coates have looked at in their comments: if ecstasy is now pluralised and around in many sites and many functions, and if it is not so much an arbiter of any building type, like the church or even the museum, the question – which is a rather nasty question, but I must raise it – is whether you can have ecstasy without taboo?

Paul Finch May I remind you all about the distinction between the erotic and kinky. The erotic is when you draw a feather across the skin of your beloved; the kinky is when the whole chicken is involved.

Charles Jencks The part and the whole. The definition of a fetish is, from a psychological point of view, when you confuse the part with the whole. You fixate on the part. Having written about fetishism in architecture, I did a little research, and I found this sad tale, with which I will now depress you. It is the story of a certain kind of bird – a herring-gull – which pecks at its mother. It is born with this instinct. It pecks right around the mouth, because there the mother bird has little spots. If it pecks at the mouth, the offspring will be given a pre-digested piece of ready-made good food. The problem is that if you make this sign of a beak and the dots around it, and give it to a baby programmed with the right instinct, the baby herring-gull would rather peck at the fetish, ie the small substitute that is part of the whole, than its real mother. So attracted to the super-sign of ecstasy is this gull, that it will die of starvation. The mother, as if to get even in some heaven of fetishes, is attracted to little round objects which have the right colour spots, and will sit on these endlessly. However, if you make a super-sign to four times the size of its normal egg, and paint it with bigger dots – again part of the whole – the mother will leave her real eggs and sit on the fetish, and all her small offspring will die, not having even pecked at her mouth. This is a sad tale of ecstasy.

Robert Maxwell Who is giving us humans these outsized eggs? Where are they coming from? Why am I constantly attracted towards them?

Charles Jencks Well, that is what taboo has something to tell us about. If the shock of the new shocks, it must be new and a taboo. You said – I am quoting you quoting me – ecstasy is where the new becomes visible; so you are attracted, even in spite of yourself to that.

Charles Jencks

Our skin is nothing more than another type of osmotic membrane to a variety of human technologies. We view ourselves continuously from without – this is the ecstasy of the Millennium and its architectures are ecstatic architectures.

Neil Spiller

Ecstacity
Nigel Coates

David Lachapelle's Emmanuel as Angel *is a reminder that ecstasy was first expressed as a religious experience*

The unbuilt proposal for the 1964 New York World Fair captures the clichéd image of ecstasy as explosion

A few years ago I designed an exhibition called *Ecstacity*, which explored how information technology could bring desire into architecture. I had become interested in this word 'ecstasy' when reading Jean Baudrillard's comments on communication excess and how it saturates the world we live in. He referred to an ecstasy of communication – critically. I thought – if we live in this saturated world, then we ought to get used to it and start enjoying it.

Ecstasy: the dictionary definition ranges from 'frenzy' to 'rapture', which is something much gentler. So it is about a loss of control, giving up your reliance on order in a space. But it is also about passion – David Lachapelle's *Emmanuel as Angel* is an ironic contemporary image, but one that certainly illustrates the fact that ecstasy has been associated with religious experience, hence its imagery, sculptures and churches.

In a wider urban context, a city is a brutal, tough place where some people have to live in cardboard boxes, but ecstatic experience is one of its promises too. Aside from the legendary stress of the city, within it lies the potential for ecstatic moments – triggered by signs, conditions or feelings. You can set up these increments of ecstasy, as I do everyday on my

motorbike ride to work, or react to effort built into our surroundings to trigger ecstasy within us. Hot spots of potential ecstasy tantalise us from all around – advertisements promise something; an ecstatic experience that comes with the goods.

I think that ecstasy, or at least its representation, is now key to the contemporary language of advertising. It goes with consumerism because it is its flip side. In graphics and contemporary imagery we more or less demand the impossible be experienced as though it were real, like the Pink Floyd album cover in which two men shake hands while one of them is on fire. Perhaps in associating with the product or the music there is some notion of a promised ecstatic experience. We have come a long way from nineteenth-century notions that the sites of ecstasy can be confined to religion or art.

In architecture there are sophisticated examples of shaping ecstatic potential, as in the proposal for Spiral to the Stars for the 1964 New York World Fair, which was a very frank, almost clichéd, graphic demonstration of an ecstatic experience that expresses some notion of the universe. Similarly, leisure places not only promise an ecstatic experience, but improve upon the real thing. At a bathing park in Japan, a glorious beach just minutes from it is deserted, whereas the new island is completely 'built', the waves are artificial, and so on. So (un)real oceans around the world are more dependably ecstatic than the (unpredictable) sea.

Ecstasy can be added to the city as a form of decoration as statuary on top of buildings, or as an ephemeral transgression like fire-works. For Houston's bicentennial celebration, a collective ecstasy was achieved by the usual skyline being replaced by the fireworks that sprang from it. Back in London's Soho, the Harley Davidsons line up on a Thursday night to produce a different sort of ecstatic contrivance; that of pushing the narrow streets to their limit, with the strength of the pack, the invasion of the (quiet) street. It seems that it is in the nature of cities that they will look for moments of ecstatic possi-bility. So the city has a capacity to stage this ecstasy in all sorts of unexpected ways.

I remember how the moment before an Alexander McQueen fashion show held an incredibly dense expectation of a pleasure that was about to follow. It reminded me of Fellini's films, of certain exaggerations of the scale of the Royal Horticultural Hall, but with the crowds of photographers at the bottom creating a magical atmos-

Water World in Japan builds a complete paradise only yards from the real beach

Jean Michel Jarre's staging of Houston's Bicentennial celebra-tions converted office towers into giant roman candles

The Felliniesque atmosphere before the start of an Alexander McQueen show

phere that is necessary for the ecstatic space to work. An architect can also contrive this ecstatic anticipation, as in Rem Koolhaas' drawing of the downtown New York Athletic Club, where the improbability of eating oysters, nude, with boxing gloves, somehow promises ecstasy. There is a certain ecstasy in reading the image itself. Carlo Mollino's beautiful garconniere may not be as visceral as oysters but it is certainly liquid: the space flows uninterrupted over padded walls offering glimpses from one room to another. There is a certain erotic charge in being able to slip between spaces with a notion of ecstasy as the final reward.

It may be unwise to say that we can create ecstatic spaces artificially, as did those people with a high drug consumption. It is fundamental, surely, this aspect of the city. The city has as many desires as the number of its inhabitants; they come together at certain moments, as in night clubs, for example.

Nevertheless, there is a space – due to the drug – to the music, to the people themselves, to the container and finally to the knowledge that this is a special place, a special zone in which an ecstatic experience is very likely to occur. But ecstasy in architecture is more to do with the rapturous than the frenzied – I have explored the potential for architecture to trigger this, by being open to the emphasis of the feelings that an individual experiences, rather than power.

It is easy to see that there is a sense of delight in the improbable, the anti-gravitational, the dynamic;

In Carlo Mollino's Casa Devalle, 1939, space flows uninterrupted over padded walls

A naked figure mirrors the contours of a rolling landscape

these are objectives of frenzied ecstasy in architecture. Let us take the frenzy out of ecstasy for the moment, look at the rapture, slow things down. Let us look at the body as a means of receiving and transmitting this ecstatic experience, as in these images related to ecstasy. The preceding project for King's Cross is more frenzied, and about the pasting and layering and constant transformation from one sort of urban activity to another.

An early scheme of ours in Japan, Caffè Bongo, was inspired by Fellini's *La Dolce Vita*. It is an example of the transparency between the glamorous events that are portrayed in the film and the extraordinarily rich background of Rome which we tried to reflect in this particular design.

An early version of what I came to call Ecstacity combines the image of the body and the much larger scale of the city itself. So when *Vogue* asked me to make a sandcastle – Ron Arad and several other architects constructed one also – I tried to build what was not just a castle but a city. There is a River Thames in the foreground. Somehow the idea of a sleeping figure, the rapturous giant, representing another scale; another aspect of the city experience, became embedded. A model of Big Ben is suggested and maybe Hampstead is that lobster pot at the back.

The 1992 *Ecstacity* exhibition at the Architectural Association suggested that certain elements of the city could be swapped, a bit like dominoes. There were videos of different urban conditions and then

*Branson Coates' Eurofields project
for the Metropolis show at the
ICA, London, 1988, encouraged
the constant transformation of
one activity into another*

*Caffè Bongo, 1986, one of Branson
Coates' earliest projects in Japan,
mixed trash and glamour*

huge paintings at the back, which showed how a city could express a desire to evolve and to formulate new conditions with spaces that add on to those already in existence. The River Thames moved into Somerset House, Terry Farrell's Embankment Place grew a huge platform: wing-like spaces slipped over the Strand and on to Covent Garden, and so on – growth and evolution.

This project led to drawings of what might happen to the Thames for the Millennium, using quite crude computer graphics to paste new formats on top of the existing ones. Again, there was a sense of becoming, of evolution, of everything metamorphosing, the kind of elasticity of which Paolo Portoghesi speaks. At a smaller scale, one sees the way that the advertisement on the Strand Theatre steps into the road and becomes the facade of a building or new buildings invade the Strand – as do these two coffee houses.

Another project, for Times Square in New York, uses the fact that the image-saturated containment of that space is a kind of urban nightclub, in which the relationship between the figure in space and the surrounding images form the architecture. These, rather than the buildings, could be accentuated by making a live connection to an equivalent space on the other side of the world, twelve hours away in Tiananmen Square. So while there are plenty of Calvin Klein advertisements, there is also the live connection to Tiananmen Square. It is a parallelism that is

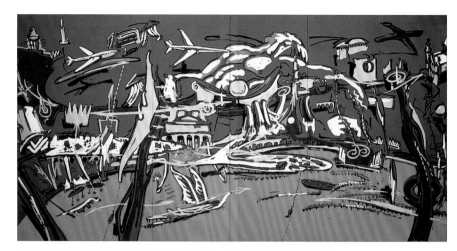

ABOVE: Branson Coates' 1992 project, Ecstacity, added a soft, responsive architecture to the familiar terrain of imperial central London

CENTRE AND BELOW: A later version of Ecstacity as a millennial art park tunes and transforms the Thames

Ecstacity moves on to Times Square in New York, proposing a live link to Tiananmen Square, which is exactly twelve hours time difference away

Two coffee houses frame this church in the Strand, London: a small ecstatic add-on

about motion and change at the rapturous end of the ecstatic spectrum.

Our project for the Bankside Bridge in London, which is being built by Norman Foster, is a demonstration of an object that has a sense of becoming, of change, and in that sense it invites an ecstatic experience, much closer to the work of Borromini than Bernini. It does not so much represent ecstatic experience as induce it.

Meanwhile, the bridge that we designed for the *Living Bridges* exhibition as part of the competition that was held in conjunction with it, was never intended to be as frankly erotic as it turned out to be; but people were very quick to see it like this. On the inside of that bridge, various platforms are intended to create an experience that is very arterial and constantly transforming; where one level suddenly turns out to be on another.

The *Erotic Design* exhibition at the Design Museum was a more deliberate ecstatic space. At the interior level it actually borrowed some motifs from Mollino, such as wavy curtains. The show included various pieces of his furniture, the Allen Jones pieces, and an extraordinary motorbike, all illustrating figures living 'ecstatically' in objects.

The Oyster House, which recently won a competition, arises from the same agenda of 'ecstatic' metamorphosis and change. It is related strongly to a sense of the inside being connected to the outside. In fact, the Oyster House is quite symmetrical and logical in plan; it has a platform, which is like

ABOVE: *Branson Coates and Anish Kapoor's scheme for the Bankside Millennium Bridge competition transforms the axis from St Paul's into a huge spiked trajectory*

RIGHT: *The elongated spiral levels of Branson Coates' 'bridge city' are intended to undo the logic of floors and stairs*

a cross, and a very simple lower level with two staircases that cross one another. We invested the furniture with a feeling of mobility: We wished it to communicate an ability to be moved, to respond easily to needs or desires.

The National Centre for Popular Music in Sheffield also has a symmetrical plan: four drums arranged around a cross space. But the intention is close to the Baroque: for order and rapture to combine. A red tongue emerges from between two of the drums, on any one of the four sides, as a kind of tantalising sign that is reinforced by a fluorescent red path on the ground. The strange snouts on the top rotate; they are part of the ventilation system. There is a gentle sense of transformation and, on the interior, a sense of confusion and exploration which will be continued in the exhibition spaces themselves. From above it is actually a very simple geometric form, but from within, the intention is to solicit some cumulative, evolving ecstatic experience.

My current attitude to ecstasy in architecture is on this threshold between order and rapture. The concrete qualities of architecture can throw themselves open to the demands for ecstasy we make on our lives; demands we make constantly, often unconsciously.

ABOVE: Branson Coates' Oyster
House, built at the 1998 Ideal
Home show, encouraged its
inhabitants to bring change into
their lives

OPPOSITE: Sixties' objects in the
Power of Erotic Design *exhibition
at the Design Museum, London,
1997, blend mass production
with overt body form*

Branson Coates' National Centre
for Popular Music, Sheffield,
1999, has a Baroque spirit that
combines order and rapture

Body and Ecstasy
Interview with Nigel Coates

September 30, 1998

THE MILLENNIUM BODY

Charles Jencks The Millennium Body is a much more controlled celebration in ritual, partly due to necessity – to time constraints and budget. Can you describe its evolution?

Nigel Coates The original design was a semi-realistic, seated figure of indeterminate sex, with arms clasped around the left knee, and looking past a child, that was, in some way, in its care. The debates on the body were mostly centred around the question of its sex; there was a fear over whether it was male or female. Also, was it a symbol of the State, like Britannia, or was it a member of the government? What did it represent? We couldn't say: 'Oh, it's the body, as in an anatomical textbook.' Rather, it was a representation of both an individual and collective aspiration towards the next century and the millennium. I focused on one of the major trajectories in our attitudes to the body this century, the question of gender, of how men and women consider each other. In the art world, much work has been a done on the politics of the body, about claiming the body as yours; and that tipped over into the fashion world with tattooing and body adornment. These are all aspects of different attitudes towards our bodies and who we are.

Charles Jencks Adolf Loos argued that ornament, and tattooing the

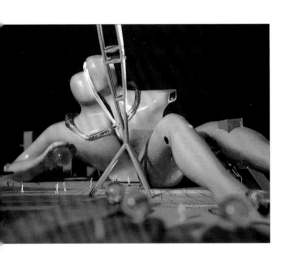

Branson Coates' Body Zone for the Millennium Dome emphasises the distinct nature of man and woman while exploring their transformation into each other. At 27 metres high, the Body Zone is itself a building which up to 4,000 people an hour will pass through

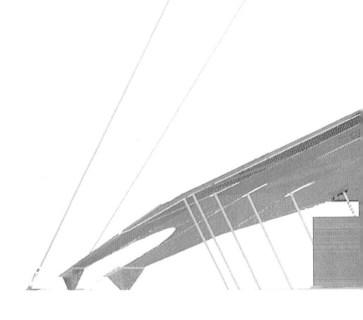

body, is regression, and that today we don't have need of ornament and tattoo because we have higher pleasures, abstract pleasures. Anyone who tattoos their body, he said, is either a degenerate aristocrat or a criminal. In resurrecting the body and ornament you have gone against one of the foundations of Modernism.

Nigel Coates Le Corbusier looked at the body as a symbol, as a measure, all the things we have talked about, but not as a unit of feeling or pleasure . . .

Charles Jencks Which is why this country has been wound up over the sex of the millennium figure. It has been both titillating and a hard question to answer. Your solution is not only hermaphroditic, but it could also be read as a couple engaged in play and sex, or at least embracing. I understand you have consciously designed a reclining rather than dominating figure, an avoidance of the power figure, the Colossus.

Nigel Coates Yes, we don't want a Nazi or Stalinist type of figure. We want to use the contrast in scale between the figure and that of the working parts of the building like the columns, lifts and, of course, the visitors, as though the representation were a benign giant that resides in the landscape of the city . . . very much an idea that I first started to explore in the 'Ecstacity' work.

The Dissolving, Floating, Exploding Architecture of Coop Himmelb(l)au
Charles Jencks

Apparently, most people have dreams of flying unaided by a machine. The characteristic dream is rather like swimming in the air, hovering weightless above the earth and then, with outstretched arms, gliding anywhere the mind wills the body like a very fast and agile hawk. Psychoanalysts argue that this archetypal reverie has a sexual basis, presumably because arousal and orgasm sometimes result in a floating experience as natural chemicals flood the brain and the body. Many drugs also induce a similar weightless feeling, and even for a few short seconds nicotine can do the trick. Hallucinogens and sex create natural metaphors, the idea that the body is dissolving, floating, burning or even exploding. A lover might say, without giving it much thought, 'I'm consumed or bursting with passion'.

For thirty years the Viennese architects Coop Himmelb(l)au, led by Wolf Prix and Helmut Swiczinsky, have been pursuing an architecture formed on basic metaphors. They have built two works which are convincing illustrations of the way we respond emphatically to the genre of naturally expressive signs. Within the area of Ecstatic Architecture they are a particular type, on the frenzied, rather than the serene, end of the spectrum.

Rooftop Remodelling, Vienna, 1983–88

Rooftop office conversion, Vienna, 1984–86

Their works are explosive rather than sublime, tough not soothing. As sexual metaphor they are the build-up to fulfilment rather than the afterglow of Saint Teresa's swoon.

The Rooftop remodelling in Vienna scampers all over the top of a conventional, Classical block as if it were a pterodactyl searching out a victim. The bird image is partly acknowledged but, as in all Coop Himmelb(l)au's work, no single metaphor is really adequate. Many ideas smash through each other, accidents are incorporated as essential elements, the contingent is as important as the basic structure. In this sense, their buildings illustrate a fundamental aspect of nature: that any species is always a strange mixture of universal forces and historical accident. Complexity Theory has recently unravelled such dualities, the fruitful disposition located at the 'edge of chaos' where order and disorder together can lead to the emergence of genuine novelty. Coop Himmelb(l)au's architecture is very much on the chaotic side of this balance.

Order is challenged by a superior disorder. The Viennese Rooftop explosion has a basic organisational backbone, a taut arc shape and a glass skylight that both lean over the edge of the roof. But crystalline planes of various sorts have their own different orders, so that the totality is always moving, always tense with excitement. One doesn't quite know where to focus, the eye is always led to another fractured explosion of glass and white structure. Lighting dissolves boundaries,

Rooftop, exterior view

crystal geometries penetrate each other, jagged shapes skewer the skin, walls merge as in a dream. The interior conference room is one of the great set-pieces of Prix's kind of architecture, too quickly pigeon-holed as Deconstructivist.

It is true that the structure questions itself and denies some of its load-bearing role, visually that is, and it is not consistent. But the effects are playful not analytic, expressive rather than conceptual, closer to Expressionist Architecture than to the cerebral machinations of Bernard Tschumi or Peter Eisenman. They remind one of an early characterisation of Duchamp's *Nude Descending a Staircase*: 'an explosion in a shingle factory'. Fragmentation and dissonance there may be, but it is symphonic and ecstatic.

The recently completed UFA Cinema Centre in Dresden is also a joyful explosion of planes. Part of this has a rational base or at least, as described by Wolf Prix, an economic rationalisation: it takes functional advantage of the canti-lever to release ground space that is more expensive than air rights. Eight cinema theatres are canti-levered in one block and a crystal, glass shell wraps up a wandering public space. Prix returns again and again to the metaphors of free or open space, 'liberated space carved out of the air', as if it was a volume of the public realm open to every-body, as free as the air we breathe. For him, as for the traditional European architect, the role of the architect is to celebrate the public realm, literally to crystallise freedom

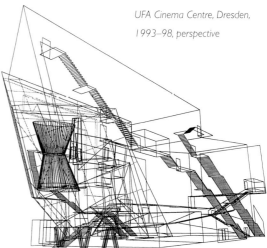

UFA Cinema Centre, Dresden, 1993–98, perspective

as an explosion of light. Yet there is an interesting inversion here. If Le Corbusier's concrete architecture celebrated 'the masterly, correct and magnificent play of volumes in light', then Coop Himmelb(l)au's work does the reverse. Thus it is best seen in twilight when interior lights masterfully break up the volumes into suspended shades of glowing planes. The elevator core leans this way and that; bridges, stairs and ramps fly past each other at indeterminate distance. There are no boundaries, no closure, no endings.

Prix talks about the space defined not by axes and monuments, but by tangents, vectors and diagonals. Seen from the exterior, the crystalline walls lean out precariously, following several geometries of different mullion grids. Order is here, the order of a collapsing ice-floe, a crystal growing out to one side with self-similar shapes. To the other side the blank concrete tilts of the auditoria rake up and loom out in an equally ominous cantilever. It is a threatening frenzy, a tough industrial version of ecstasy, perhaps a Dionysian rapture. Or is it hypersex without love? Only the hanging 'skybar', a double-cone designed with the artist Kiki Smith, provides an harmonious, rounded shape to all the stark angularities. Current critical discourse might classify this as the fashionable 'Sadean dismemberment of the body', but that kind of analysis misses the point.

This, after all, is a media centre with eight cinemas, and going to the movies is meant to provide an exhilarating and certainly unusual

UFA Cinema Centre, light dissolves volumes

experience. Disjunctive, cataclysmic, even orgasmic architecture is thinkable in this context. Film is the most shifting and dissolvable of all media. It is the one into which people project their lives, their bodily states, their hopes and fears – if only for a moment.

The building takes on the feelings of this experience: 'architecture as frozen cinema' if you will. Liquid, dissolving, floating, fractured montage. The ritual of mounting a long gangway, entering a dark room and watching a movie may not be the same as Cro-Magnon man going inside a cave to experience the flickering light illuminate paintings of charging bulls. The latter was part of a larger experience meant to connect the onlooker with supernatural powers, yet both film and cave painting can induce feelings of being transported to another realm outside this world, and the anti-gravity architecture of Coop Himmelb(l)au, while ultra-real in its hard-tech, creates sensations of vertiginous flight.

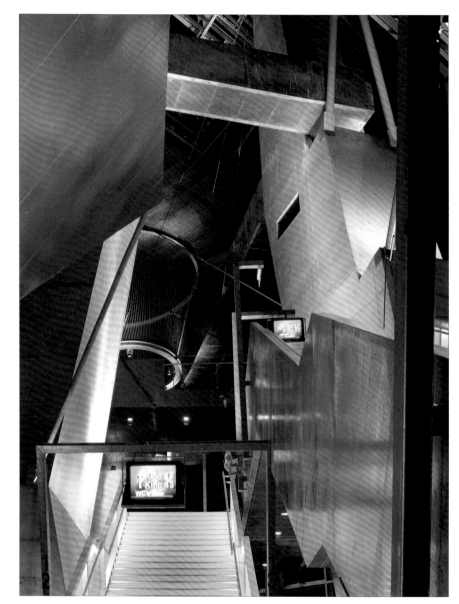

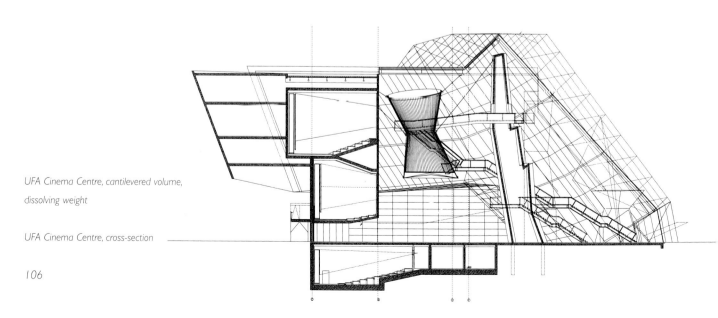

UFA Cinema Centre, cantilevered volume, dissolving weight

UFA Cinema Centre, cross-section

THE DISSIPATION OF OUR BODIES IN THE CITY

WE LOVE TO DESIGN (THE) LINES AND SURFACES OF THE CITY, THE ONES THAT DO NOT EXIST YET. TO DISCOVER AND VISIBLY DRAW THE ONES THAT ARE INVISIBLE. JUST AS WE LOVE TO BUILD BUILDINGS AND THEIR SHADOWS.

IN RECENT YEARS — SINCE ABOUT 1978 — WE BEGAN — WITHOUT KNOWING WHERE IT WOULD LEAD US TO — TO DENSITY AND SHORTEN THE TIME OF THE DESIGN PROCESS. THAT'S TO SAY, DISCUSSIONS ABOUT THE PROJECT ARE CERTAINLY HELD AT LENGTH. BUT ALWAYS WITHOUT THINKING OF SPATIALLY CONCEIVABLE CONSEQUENCES. AND THEN SUDDENLY: THE DRAWING IS THERE. ON THE WALL, ON THE TABLE, ON A PIECE OF PAPER.

SOMEWHERE.

AND ALWAYS AND SIMULTANEOUSLY THERE IS THE MODEL (IN NO SCALE).

THIS IS HOW IT WORKS: COOP HIMMELBLAU IS A TEAM. THERE ARE TWO OF US. WHILE DRAWING, ARCHITECTURE IS CAPTURED IN WORDS, THE DRAWING IS NARRATED INTO THE THREE-DIMENSIONAL MATERIAL OF THE MODEL. (WE CAN'T PROVE IT, BUT WE SURMISE VERY STRONGLY THAT THE MORE INTENSELY THE DESIGN IS EXPERIENCED BY THE DESIGNER, THE BETTER THE BUILT SPACE WILL BE EXPERIENCED.)

LAST YEAR WE NOTICED THAT WE GRADUALLY BEGAN TO EMPHASISE THE VERBAL DESCRIPTION OF THE DESIGN WITH GESTURES OF OUR HANDS. AND WITH PROJECTS FROM PARIS AND VIENNA, THE LANGUAGE OF THE BODY WAS THE BETTER DRAWING AND THE FIRST MODEL.

AND WHEN WE BEGAN TO WORK ON THE PROJECTS FOR THE CITIES NEW YORK AND BERLIN, THE FACE AND BODY OF THESE CITIES BECAME MORE AND MORE DISTINCT: ON A TEAM PHOTO OF COOP HIMMELBLAU, WE BEGAN TO SEE AND DRAW THE LINES AND SURFACES OF THE CITY. OUR EYES BECAME TOWERS, OUR FOREHEADS BRIDGES, THE FACES BECAME LANDSCAPES, AND OUR SHIRTS SITE-PLANS.

SUPERIMPOSING THE EXISTING CITY MAP AND THE NEW DRAWING, THE CONTOURS, LINES AND SURFACES OF THE FACES AND BODIES, PREVIOUSLY SO IMPORTANT, GRADUALLY VANISHED IN THE WHIRL OF EXISTING PLANNING. YET THE LINES, FIELDS AND SURFACES OF THE NEW STRUCTURE DELINEATE THEMSELVES CLEARLY, EVER MORE CLEARLY. THEY BECAME THREE DIMENSIONAL AND CAST SHADOWS.

NOW WE ARE GOING TO ENLARGE OUR TEAM PHOTO, STEP BY STEP, UNTIL JUST THE PUPILS OF THE EYES ARE VISIBLE. THEY ARE THE PLAN OF A TALL BUILDING, AND WE INTEND TO BUILD IT.

COOP HIMMELBLAU (1988)

Alsop & Störmer

Aesthetic Perception: The Subject of Architecture

Charles Jencks

Will Alsop, like Frank Gehry, is an architect who keeps one foot firmly planted in the world of art. His projects shown here are painted and modelled, as Gehry's are, in order to discover new possibilities latent in the language of architecture. In this sense, they are a combination of invention and research, an extension of architectural knowledge at a sensual level.

In my last essay on Gehry, I have tried to capture this double endeavour with neologisms – 'cognerotic', 'sensuolect' – because it is so important and no word can describe it adequately. The duality is based on two deep instincts which are operative at once, and thereby synergetic.

Alsop, like Greg Lynn, extends architectural knowledge with two motifs that can be seen here: the flexible net and the warped blob. When his work becomes a heightened sign of these aesthetic-technical concerns, when buildings become 'architecture about aesthetic perception', then, as usual, they tend towards the euphoric and the ecstatic.

WILL ALSOP – ARCHITECTURE'S EDGES

. . . 'Great architecture is good for you'. It has the ability to relieve stress, empower the individual, and be beautiful, and yet, it is under-valued everywhere.

Architecture is not merely *buildings*.

Architecture = building +

Plus what?

The 'what is' thing, like time and space, has no actual physical properties. It should not be con-fused with the architectural object. It is the subject of architecture which has properties that transcend the physicality of the object.

The subject of *architecture* is aesthetic perception. Some archi-tects talk of the subject requiring rigour. It does, but not in the con-stipated form of their interpretation. It is not a discipline that reduces elements to a mannerist set of principles. Architecture is an inquiry and it is the discovery of architecture through inquiry which requires rigour . . .

Expo 2000 Pavilion, Hanover,
1998, exterior perspective

Hotel du Départment, 'Le Grand
Bleu', Marseilles, 1993–94

*Expo 2000 Pavilion, interior
perspective*

Warped net structure

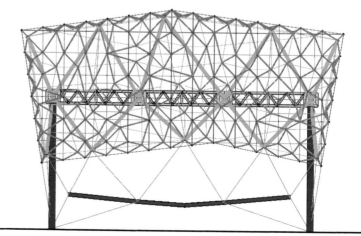

EXPO 2000 PAVILION, HANOVER, 1998

The building is both container and experience, acting on the Expo site as a landmark. From a distance, the building excites curiosity and draws people towards it. It is layered so that the eye cannot rest on either the exterior or the interior.

The envelope is constructed of a lightweight inflated membrane which can vary its translucence by altering the pressure within the cushion layers. This controls the heat gain of the building, as well as creating an ever-changing envelope. In addition, light water sprays on the external envelope to create a mist which gives the illusion that the building is slightly out of focus.

Physically, the building is intended as a demountable and adaptive structure. Central to its structure is a large moving crane which allows the building to construct itself and bring in large and changing exhibits within its cathedral like internal space.

The building is constructed of four primary elements: a large demountable four-legged steel 'table', which forms the primary structure; a large conical steel 'spider' structure, spanning above and below the table, tensioned by a network of cables; a matrix of inflated ETFE cushions on a 3.5 x 3.5 metre grid, dressed over the 'spider' structure, to form an insulated and transparent envelope; and a cable structure, hanging below the table structure that supports a floor which floats above ground level.

Expo 2000 Pavilion, model

Longitudinal section

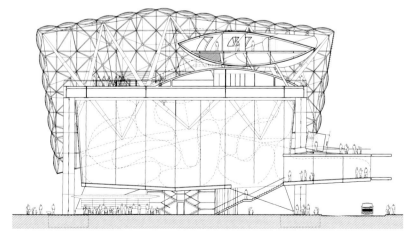

INSTITUTE OF CONTEMPORARY ARTS
(ICA), LONDON, 1996

At first we considered relocating
the ICA on the Jubilee Garden site.
The institute was interpreted as a
square, gridded landscape which is
penetrated by free-form objects
enclosing the galleries, auditorium
and restaurant facilities. In a second
phase we considered another river
location alongside Blackfriar's
Bridge.

An important consideration in
the design of the building at
Blackfriar's has been the height and
headroom restrictions imposed by
the Port of London Authority, due
to the clear headroom required
over the shipping lane of the River
Thames and the planning restrictions
related to the views of Saint Paul's
Cathedral. The shape of the building
is a clear result of maximising the
internal volume within these height
restrictions.

The accommodation is organised
largely on three levels above
ground. The floor below ground
contains mainly services and work-
shops; the upper levels contain
mainly the major public spaces;
and the ground floor serves
primarily as the building entrance.
Building features include a theatre,
gallery and cinema planning, which
are up-to-date and adaptable.

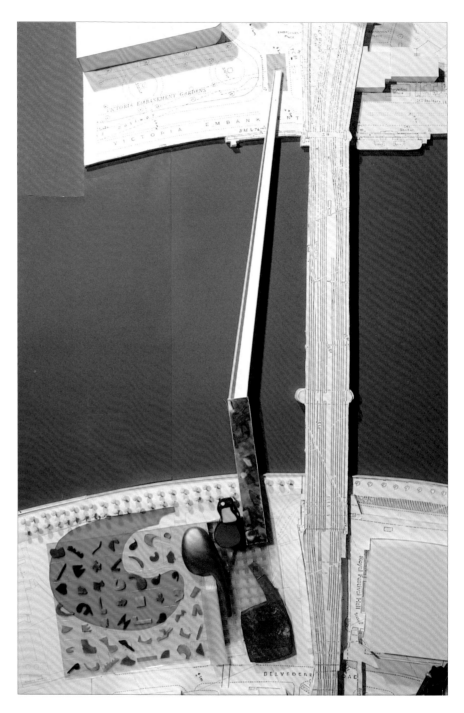

Institute of Contemporary Arts,
site plan, Jubilee Garden

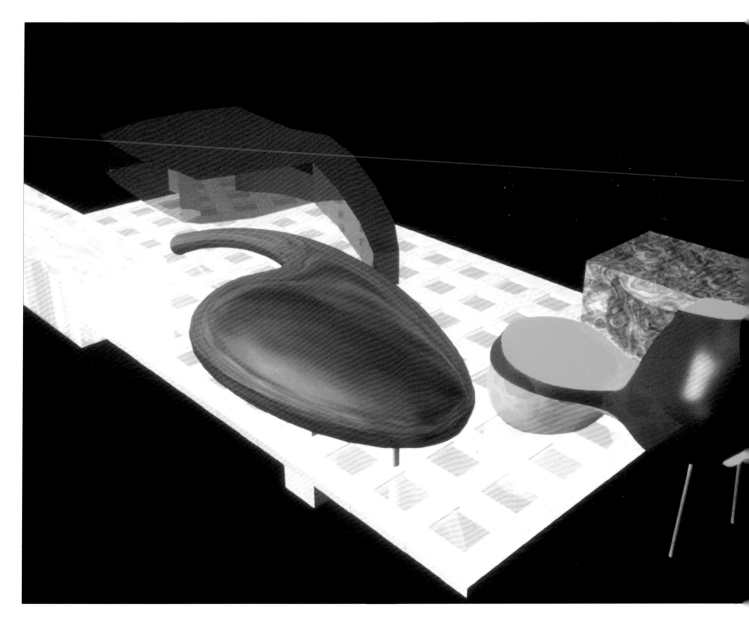

Institute of Contemporary Arts, aerial view of model

The Jersey Café, St Helier, Jersey, 1998

Stealthily Fluid (Moving) Spaces
Odile Decq

French Expo Pavilion, Venice, 1996

Paul Virilio said to his students that after the Functionalistic revolution of the first part of the twentieth century, with its abstract, rationalistic solutions, and following on from the emergence of a new society in the second part of the century when social needs were met by quantitative social solutions, architecture today has to answer the question of desire in terms of giving pleasure. This does not mean that the question of function and needs disappears but rather that these issues are basic architectural obligations that have to be normatively resolved. It is the fundamental statement of all architecture, yet fufilling the call to satisfy such desire is complex. Each answer has to be specific and significant. Nothing is definitive, every solution is transitory.

These notions of satisfying desire question the place of the body and the senses in space and architecture. The displacement of the body inside space, the instability generated by movement, the instability which creates movement, these change our way of perceiving space through our senses. After rendition of the body as stable throughout the Classical periods, where space is perceived from a static point, we are now in the dynamic period in which the body is perceived as unstable, where time and space are seen as instants,

as events instead of permanencies. We enter a nomadic period in which the discontinuity of space and the fracture of time is a modern condition.

Speed, movement and displacement are the modern conditions of sensual pleasure in space and time. The disappearance of predefined forms, of precise limits, characterises the evolution of architecture based on movement. The Quattrocento perspective statically oriented away from the viewer cannot express the chaotic disorder and fragmentation of today's urban space, nor the unfolding of the axes of communication, the multiple paths of new sensuality, nor respond to our new perception of time and space.

Movement becomes an ordering principle and we adapt ourselves to the perception of cityscape and space while in motion. The architecture of these new territories, in which man is in a state of constant displacement, where the meaning and perception of time constantly redefine our perception of space, could be perceived as imperfect, non-limiting and evolving.

The modern urban space is definitely not in the order of the city: the notion of place to movement, to elision, to continuous displacement of places and activities. Territory is no longer defined by its boundaries but by the network and

Highway Operation Centre,
Nanterre, 1993

Highway viaduct, Carrière sur
Seine, Nanterre, 1993

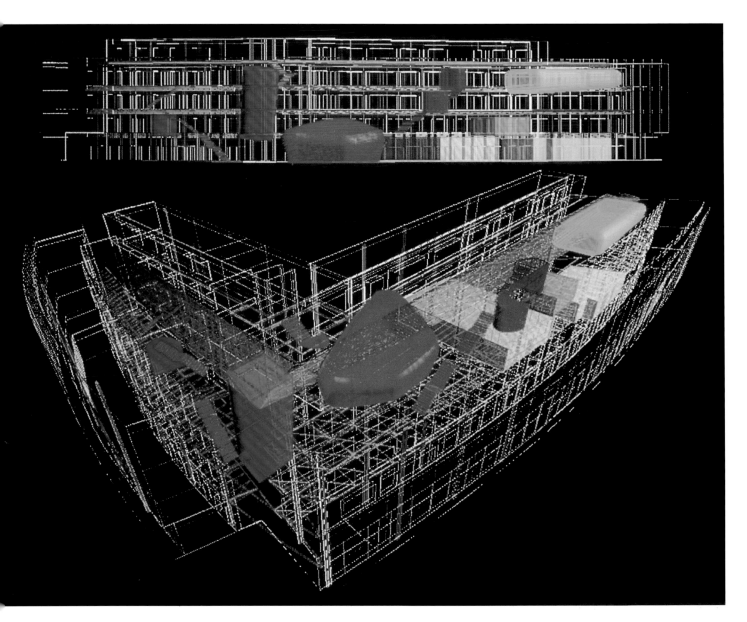

National Centre of Agriculture
and Exploitation Developments,
Limoges, 1994

the connections inside it. Territory is now always polycentric. The displacement inside cities and territories redefines them as a network in a state of continuous flux. We have to question the static spatiality and permanence of the urban form in time.

So, architecture thought as event, as instant, as interaction and network is perhaps a more efficient response to today's society than an architecture of permanence. The questions of foundation and gravity, of stability and permanence, of perspective and Euclidean geometry have to be rethought if we want, as architects, to allow people to be comfortable in this new environment.

The question of perception is fundamental in a world in which mobility achieved through displacement and moving image restructures our point of view as observers of forms and volumes, of interior and exterior space. The experience of travelling and viewing has become mobile and dynamic.

The developments of cutting, montage and the moving camera in films eliminate the unity of space and replace it with an artificial unity of time. The moving camera changes the spatial depth of the perceived world into a phenomenon of time, so falsifying and manipulating dimensions. Simultaneously, networks and faster displacements give us a cinematic and global view of the world. This creates the chaos of images that confronts us with a world that has lost its materiality and dimension and has been de-realised.

The connection of car, plane and camera, the evolution of

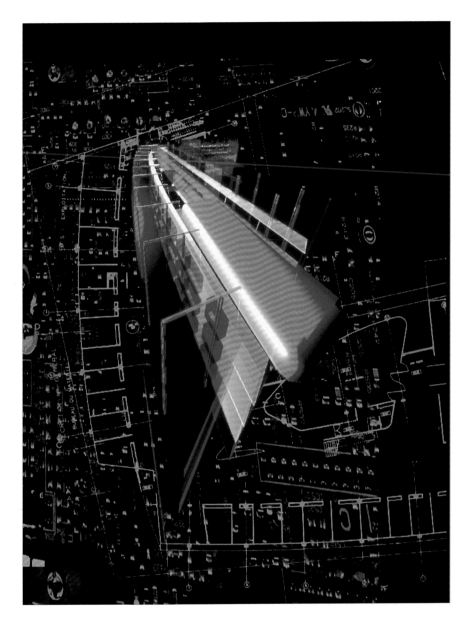

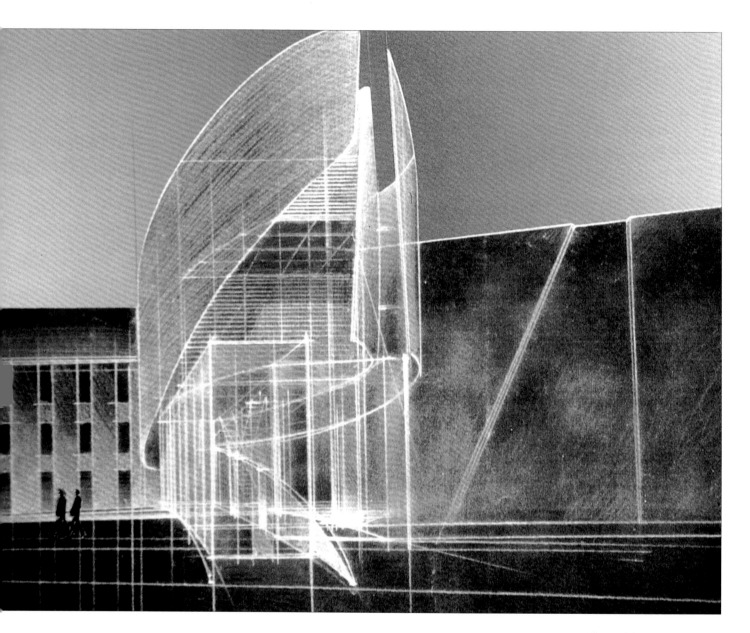

*Centre of Contemporary
Creation, Tours, 1993*

sophisticated instruments of perception, have revolutionised the space–time of seeing. We must think about the possibility of a new kind of gravity, or machine of gravity, that understands the relativity of the moment of perception.

The variation of perspectives creates a permanent tension and a sensual ambiguity in complexity and perception of space. The sequential articulation of images such as linear distortion constantly displaces and perturbs the point of view. Material, light, texture, colours, just as form, shadow, tension, density, movement, transgression, hypertrophy, all are our combined tools to create spaces in which the senses are awakened. Architecture and space are related in a constant process of discovery and are never out of bounds.

Ron Arad
Ecstatic Architecture Symposium
The Royal Academy of Arts, London

These stills are from a patchwork of home videos that we made recently.

The first exercise, a blind date with tempered steel in a workshop at the Vitra Design Museum, was concerned with the flexibility of material and fuelled a lot of work, both in architecture and with objects.

In RTW (Reinventing the Wheel), we made use of gravity rather than material to help us. This is a rare example of a project in which computer animation was done after the event. It is a life drawing. Usually, we work the other way round.

In our competition entry for the Making the Modern World gallery at the Science Museum in London, the main exhibition floor moves so slowly that it is almost imperceptible; turntables set into the surface of the floor rotate the exhibits. The gallery forms the main route to the new Wellcome wing. On viewing it again, when leaving the museum an hour or so after having entered, visitors find the room layout has changed. In the same project, an information-rich balustrade allows visitors to find out about the history behind the objects in the gallery.

Tempered steel, Vitra Design Museum, 1991

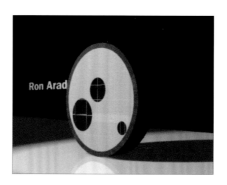 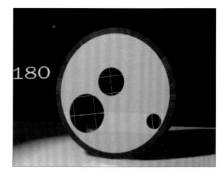

Reinventing the Wheel, 1996

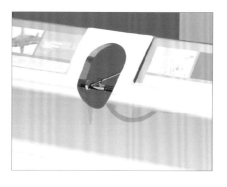 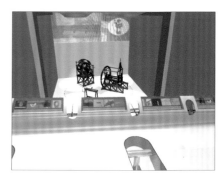

Modern World Gallery, Science Museum, London, 1997

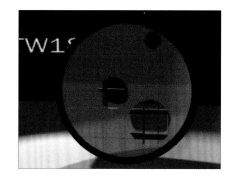 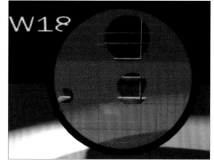 

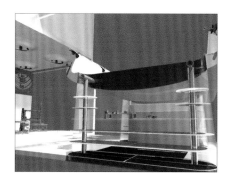  

The Achenbach Gallery in Dusseldorf takes advantage of the concrete structural columns of the building to cantilever pivoting walls which rotate to create different spaces.

The installation made for the opening of Jean Nouvel's Cartier Foundation in Paris was a very big gamble. No elaborate drawings were required, merely one of the table and five minutes of spatial organisation; the rest was just 'wait and see'. I came three days before the exhibition, but there was nothing left for me to do. The space changes considerably when it is populated by people.

We filed a planning application for the Amiga House last summer and were ecstatic to gain the support of English Heritage. The house is almost rectilinear in form. It could have been built as a piece of minimalist Japanese architecture. The two outer shells are dropped in, locking the space between them.

The Adidas Stadium on the Champs Elysées in Paris evolved from the brief to design a flagship store for Adidas. A slice of the underbelly of the cinema is reflected by mirrored side walls in the entrance, creating a virtual stadium. Visitors to the shop acquire a new set of legs as they cross the entrance bridge by means of liquid crystal displays built into the balustrade. In the depths of the store, the world's largest scoreboard provides updated results twenty-four hours a day from all over the globe.

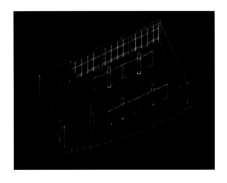 

Flying Walls, Achenbach Gallery, Dusseldorf, 1995

Amiga House, 1997

Adidas Stadium, Paris, 1996

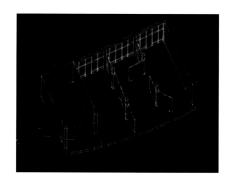

Installation for Jean Nouvel's Cartier Foundation,
Paris, 1994

Our design for the Tel Aviv Opera House makes use of a recti-linear box on the outside; the shells on the inside this time. We had to work with a space that was very strange to us. The potential came from its size, which was immense, and was therefore able to accommodate three autonomous structures.

Tel Aviv Opera House, 1994

Ron Arad

Forms of Ecstasy – Part II *Charles Jencks*
BRUCE GOFF AND GEOMETRISM

Bruce Goff takes over where Frank Lloyd Wright leaves off, at the point where underlying geometry breaks out and becomes obsessive or, to apply a neologism, 'Geometrism'. He does not, however, conform to a single pattern, but uses several compatible ones. Thus his Bavinger House, a basic spiral coiling up to an off-centre mast, is surrounded by circles and ovoid cylinders which hang from it. The construction material, rough stone accentuated by crystalline blue glass cullet, a waste product, is anything but circular and it gives many jagged contrasts to the underlying geometry. As with Wright, the architectural control is complete, covering every surface and object in an ecstasy of total design.

Bruce Goff, Bavinger House, Norman, Oklahoma, 1951–55

Bavinger interior

The house and studio for Joe Price is equally controlled, incorporating several contrasting geometries, all versions of the hexagon, a shape which itself has an interesting property. When the hexagon is subdivided it forms six equilateral triangles, or twenty smaller ones; when extended further in one direction then another it forms lozenges. These internal and external anglers and shapes are self-similar and thus the underlying order is both unified and varied.

The Price House is a veritable orgy of crystalline tetrahedra. They culminate finials that fly out across the landscape, they hang in rows like giant, falling snowflakes, they are punched into doors as windows. Then they combine, grow in size and are covered in thick pile carpet to become a conversation pit. Just as one is growing tired of all these triangles, hexagons and their combination – trihexes – one becomes aware of some counter-themes. 'Plastic rain' hangs down over the conversation pit, white goose feathers run up into the skylight and an airy hyperboloid of green string fans lightly from wall to ceiling. Merely to list these shapes and materials is to suggest the extraordinary ambience: somewhere between do-it-yourself and Surrealism, a bachelor's pad and high art. The iridescent beads and coloured glass around the door have the quality of a painting by Gustav Klimt, who influenced Goff when he was young. On one reading, the Price House is a three-dimensional version of one of Klimt's Secessionist works, and just as engaging in its sensuality.

Bruce Goff, Joe Price House, Bartlesville, Oklahoma, 1956–76 (Price photographs courtesy Bruce Goff)

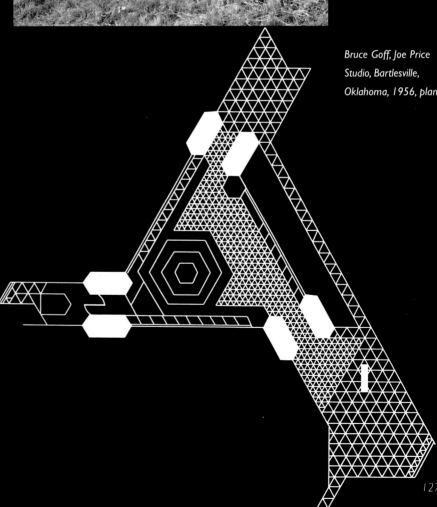

Bruce Goff, Joe Price Studio, Bartlesville, Oklahoma, 1956, plan

127

*Contrasting materials,
similar geometries*

*Price interior – the
'Klimt wall'*

FLUIDITY AND BLISS

As we have seen, there is a long historical argument for an architecture that relates to nature, its moods, lines and character. Prehistoric, Egyptian, Classical, Baroque, Art Nouveau, Organic, Expressionist and, today, Cosmogenic architecture all seek to establish links with nature in different ways. There may be no single essence to nature's inner forms. Planets and stars tend to be spheres (though there are exceptions); the Classicists conceived the universe in terms of Platonic solids (which can also be found). But, if there is an overriding language it is, as Benoit Mandelbrot has written in *The Fractal Geometry of Nature*, its self-similar forms tending to be organised in fluid, continuously changing shapes. Hence the sensual curves of the body and the fern, or the staccato, ever-moving rhythms of leaves as they group together in bundles on a tree.

Over several hundred years, the gardeners at Levens Hall in Westmoreland have fashioned uncanny topiary shapes following two of these different natural languages. On the one hand, they have cut Platonic and representational shapes out of box and yew, modifying an idea as the bushes grew and, in some cases, departing entirely from the original concept. Because of this constant reinterpretation, the results are extraordinarily fresh and sensual. On the other hand, the natural tendency for clumping and small-scale, fractal order is also evident, giving the topiary a counter-pattern and different scale. The slight changes in colour and

Monsieur Beaumont, Levens Hall, Westmoreland, seventeenth and nineteenth centuries

Erich Mendelsohn, Einstein Tower, Potsdam, 1917–21

the occasional bulbous blob that has escaped from the shears add to the feeling of sensuality. It is as if the sculpture had a will of its own and were actually alive – which it is.

With the Einstein Tower, Erich Mendelsohn sought to capture nature's viscous, fluid forms and, perhaps, Einstein's notion, extrapolated from the General Theory of Relativity, that matter bends space and time. The building was meant to ascertain whether the theory was true, but by the time it opened this was already confirmed. The question is, how much were the openings in the building a representation of the new physics? They warp, as if pulled by gravity waves, and since gravity bends light waves, that may explain why the windows are inflected. With Rudolf Steiner's Goetheanum and his idea of Anthroposophy such conjectures are on more solid ground: we know the intentions to represent nature's growing and liquid forms. Cosmic symbolism, he said, was based on the 'plastically moulded laws of nature'.

The skylights of Nicholas Grimshaw's Waterloo Station show that today the computer can control the detail and cost of fractal curves, and they modulate around a long bend, rippling like the scales of a snake.

Rudolf Steiner, Second Goetheanum, Dornach, 1924–28 (Photo

*Foreign Office Architects
(FOA), Yokohama Port
Terminal, winning com-
petition entry, 1995*

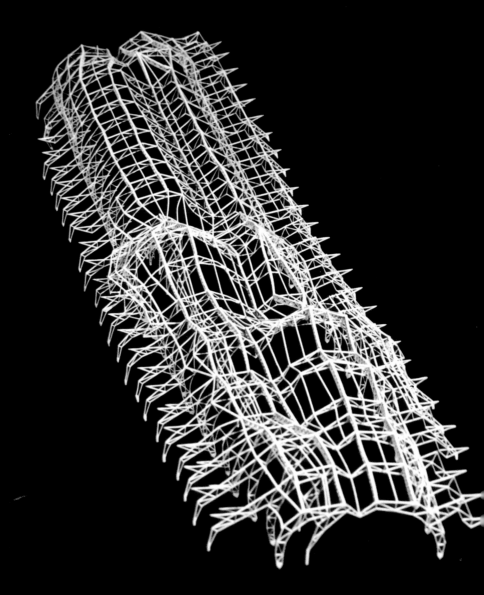

*Reiser + Umemoto,
Yokohama Port
Terminal, structural
skeleton, 1995*

Young designers, Reiser and Umemoto and Foreign Office Architects (FOA), illustrate the extent of such thinking. Steel structures can have the pliability of animals or the folded planes of geological plates and, given the new production methods, be almost as cost-effective as repetitive grids.

Andy Goldsworthy and other artists have created a land art which comes directly from natural materials – in this case packed snow, cut and laid in parabolic arches. Following the invention of Roland Penrose, I have designed several fractal structures including a rug, which is based on self-similar forms: the wide and thin rhomboid. In a true Penrose pattern, or in the quasi-crystals of nature, the overall pattern never repeats exactly.

The theme behind all this work, aside from nature, is the emphasis on holism. Bliss and rapture are states where an enveloping mood finds continuous reinforcement and variation. In these rare moments one is given over to a highly redundant ambience, where slight variations only enhance the dominant tone. Such is the state of a trance; it is very much directed from the top down, from an overall mood to the detail.

Andy Goldsworthy, Ctzise Fiord Arches, 3 April 1989

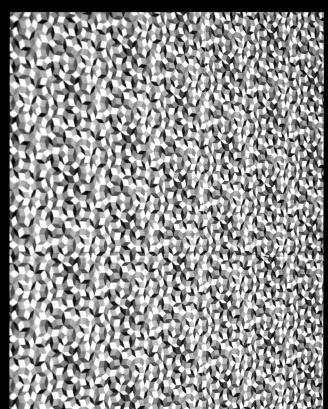

UNVEILING MYSTERY — HANS HOLLEIN

If there is a contemporary master of Ecstatic Architecture it is the Viennese architect Hans Hollein. He controls the unfolding of visual pleasure and sensual gratification as if they constituted a high drama of discovery and effects this by designing across the spectrum: architecture, interiors, sculpture, detail, art works. In this sense, he is a direct heir to Renaissance and Art Nouveau designers who were often both artist and architect. What distinguishes his work from the Baroque *Gesamtkunstwerk* is that its orientation is sexual without being religious, commercial not theocratic, although it does have a mythic component.

Hans Hollein, Retti Candle Shop, Vienna, 1965

Detail of door, lettering, Christmas wreath and veiled display window

The tiny Retti Candle Shop was his first essay in the genre and it is as sparkling, fresh and mysterious now as it was when finished more than thirty years ago. This unblemished durability results from Hollein's mastery of good materials, beautifully detailed. Flat, polished aluminium sheets are punched out and warped to give paradoxical effects. At some points the metal looks unyielding, but then it bends softly and ambiguously away from the flat plane, creating highlights and shadow in the process. Softness/hardness, skin/metal, are the contrary associations. The mythic quality stems from such opposite meanings and the absolute, bi-axial symmetry and formal ordering: it focuses on the altar and – contrary image again – the high-tech extract unit, which is treated as an icon.

Money may be the late twentieth-century religion, and shopping its daily liturgy, as many have argued, but nowhere else has this dubious idea been transformed into such high art. When I photographed the shop recently, at Christmas time in 1997, it was decked out with wreathes, putti, urns and flying hearts. The Viennese appreciate Hollein's voluptuous irony and they have commissioned four more shops in the central district which are equally worth a pilgrimage.

Retti interior with mirrors both sides doubling space

The two Schullin Jewellery Shops (one now called Caesars) are also veiled shrines which reveal themselves slowly through dense layers of symbolism. The earlier project makes a logo out of a geological form punctuated by pipes and lights. Again, the contraries are fascinating. A polished bronze 'riverbed' flows down to an 'estuary' which is layered back and into the door where it spreads into the 'sea'. All the granite, metal and glass is polished like the setting for jewellery. But this consists, in front, of mechanical ducts and light bulbs. What is going on here? One is bound to ask: if the metaphor is consistent, are they 'stepping stones'? Or, perhaps, are the fissures vaginal lips? What, anyway, is jewellery in the late high-tech twentieth century? Hollein seems to answer: an elevated form of fetishism.

What happens when you amplify this approach to large building and put it on a corner of the most important square in Vienna, opposite St Stephen's Cathedral? Hollein's Haas House is the complex result. However big the building, it is still on a very tight site with contrary pressures pushing in from both sides. Two different facade systems come from left and right, and the cathedral is across the square on the diagonal. Therefore, Hollein steps down and peels back the left facade, accommodates the right-hand context and curves out a reflective glass corner towards the religious monument. Contrasts are pushed to extremes, the opposition between a tilted Deconstructivist box and the wet-look, mirrorplate

Schullin Jewellery Shop, Vienna, 1972–74

Haas House, mixed use – shops, offices, restaurant, piazza; Vienna, 1989–90

curve being the strongest. On the inside, architectural ideas in a squashed high space are even more intense. A metallic Hollein nude seems to be doing a half-gainer, just in front of a red Chinese bridge, but the diving board from which she might have sprung is off to the right. A jumble of enticing images? Just like Christmas shopping – a surfeit of delights, sensually veiled.

Hans Hollein, a long-standing friend of mine, has provided two sketches of the phallic pillars which flank either side of the entrance to St Stephen's Cathedral. They show the left pillar surmounted by a glans penis, the right one by an open vulva; extraordinary images to welcome the fourteenth-century Catholic into church. On the inside of the cathedral the master architect pops his bemused face out of a *trompe l'oeil* door. Perhaps Freud's *The Interpretation of Dreams* can shed light on the way opposites mediate between sex and religion, but in any case it is clear that Hollein's ironic, sensual layering is deeply Viennese.

Haas House, mixed
use – shops, offices,
restaurant, piazza;
Vienna, 1989–90

Hans Hollein, sketches
of pillars, St Stephen's
Cathedral, Vienna

Hans Hollein in his
Perchtoldsdorf
conversion, 1976

MECHANOMORPHIC EROTICISM
SHIN TAKAMATSU

Origen 1, Kyoto, 1980–81

The erotic is not the ecstatic, but it certainly is a staging post on the way. The Japanese architect Shin Takamatsu has been influenced by Secession designers, such as Otto Wagner, and has also followed Hans Hollein in handling hard-edged materials in a sensuous way. Like other contemporary designers mining the same territory – Nigel Coates and Phillipe Starck – he rides a motorbike, and it shows. His work has the brilliant, mechanical eroticism of a Yamaha, the protuberant, glistening pistons of an old Bugatti, the polished massiveness of a Mack truck. It is as redundant with metal blades and polished orifices as any dragster you will find in Los Angeles. In fact, his early buildings are souped-up racing cars which just happen to be stationary.

Origen 1 (he gives buildings exotic titles) is on one reading another Face Building which focuses on the eyes and mouth, but it resembles a mechanism more than a person: perhaps the cross-section of a breached shot-gun, or one of those military robots that became

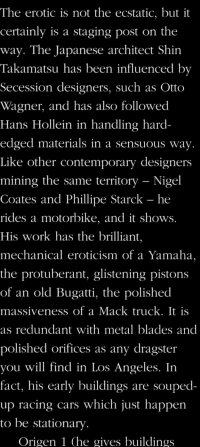

materials and integrated colours. Also, Takamatsu is quite open about the redundancy of his technology: its use and justification are very much secondary to its look.

Call it Decadent High-Tech and one invites the riposte that Takamatsu is honest about the underlying motives while others dissimulate behind function and necessity. The sheer gratuity of his techno-Expressionism is what pushes it into the realm of the ecstatic. We recognise at once where we are and can relax to enjoy the unabashed fetishism of pure materiality. This is biker's land, heavy metal music, rough-riding but no tattoos.

At Week, red metal railings and hanging trusses jump all over the grey background for the fun of the game. The visual and tactile jazz take this office and boutique out of the realm of everyday reality into the context of painting and words. Blood-red railings and capitals form a dot–dash code weaving in and out of polished aluminium struts. The syncopated composition is tough industrial music.

Week, Kyoto, 1984–86

Syntax, Kyoto, 1988

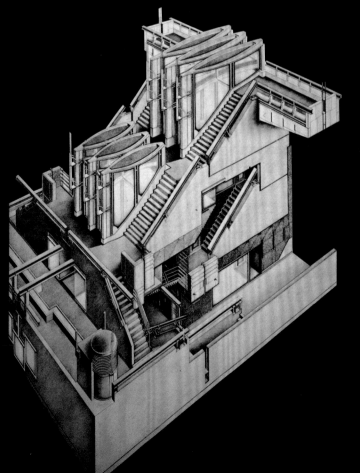

Syntax, in Kyoto, where most of these small office fantasies are built, is another vehicle that doesn't move, but it certainly seems to be trying to fly with its outstretched wings. The cantilever, as we have seen, is a hallmark of Ecstatic Architecture, because it symbolises weightlessness and out-of-body experience. It also creates vertigo and an empathetic feeling that one could actually hover in the air, effortlessly. Part of the drama in walking through and over Syntax is climbing up a route to these twin bird-perches. It is a processional, almost ritualised climb, as if one were ascending to a religious shrine such as the Temple of Heaven in Peking – except there are no sacred icons. Instead, there are beautifully detailed conjunctions of materials – granite, dovetailed aluminium, black marble orifices – and streamlined pipes that remind one of rockets and motorcycles. Whatever kind of pagan rite this may be, it culminates in the sky and a broad, expansive view over the city, a celebration of basic, cosmic pleasures.

CROSSING BOUNDARIES
FRANK GEHRY AND ERIC OWEN MOSS

A definition of Post-Modernism since the 1970s, centres on extreme hybridisation, crossing opposites, double-coding. The reason for jumping between categories and combining high and low art was obvious: to cut across the taste cultures fragmenting a pluralist society. Robert Venturi turned this into a method of combining 'complex and contradictory' elements, and Los Angeles designers Frank Gehry and Eric Owen Moss transformed it into a light-hearted and cataclysmic art. Originally, under the Greeks, one meaning of *ekstasis* was 'to be put out of place', disoriented, thrown off balance mostly in a psychic sense. In an ecstatic frenzy one does not know which passion to follow, which rule is operative; one is overwhelmed by a plethora of choice – the incongruence of many drives. It can be disturbing or creative, confusing or pleasurable. This truth has been obvious from the beginning, but its rediscovery characterises our time.

At Gloucester Cathedral, after the transept tower started to sink, pointed arches were intersected by flying buttresses. Thus two opposite systems became structurally necessary. The result is dissonant, cataclysmic and, if one is tired of easy harmonies, very interesting and pleasing. For a speculative office building in Culver City, Los Angeles, where Moss works, the opposing systems are even more pronounced. Ungainly? To be sure, but you can see Moss exults in

Gloucester Cathedral
transept buttress,
fourteenth century

Eric Owen Moss,
Culver City office,
1996

down the side it punches through the wall. All of this excessive, rhetorical contradiction has a purpose with Moss: it is to recall the past industrial aesthetic, the bowstring trusses of the previous building, and allow a continued existence in a new context, exerting a continued validity but also showing how they are equally redundant to the new requirements. The idea is that any city is a palimpsest of old and new, so the architect must both save and destroy as the new is created.

Frank Gehry's Aerospace Museum is an understated collision of functional boxes with a Lockheed F104 collaged at an angle, while his Barcelona Flying Fish is a hybridisation of several, different curved geometries.

Representational and structural requirements collide with Gehry, he starts design from opposite ends of the spectrum. But then he simplifies both so that they meld together and the characteristic result, in an office conference room, is a snake-light that coils both structurally and symbolically. It's not quite a recognisable snake, nor chandelier, but a hybrid somewhere in between. Contradiction smoothed out – on a computer one would morph one image into the other, so perhaps it should be called 'morphed contradiction'.

Frank Gehry, Aerospace Museum, Los Angeles, 1984

Frank Gehry, Flying Fish, Barcelona, 1992

Eric Owen Moss wants more angst from the collisions. His conference room in Culver City exaggerates the oppositions and shows why they are incompatible. An elliptical cone of plywood encloses the pre-existing brick space, but that and previous windows are allowed to break through and assert their rights. Old and new are not in harmony but confront each other, are made more conscious of each other's presence: 'cataclysmic contradiction'.

And so the Moss method goes, the joyful and tragic collision of geometries and cultural signs. One Culver City office block piggy-backs over an old brick structure and the trusses that carry the new sculpted shapes stick out on both sides to announce the fact. At the corner all the collisions of geometry culminate in a wonderful grey-green explosion of sensuous form seen in light and shadow. The shapes may seem arbitrary but, typically, they stem directly from practical requirements – here they are part of a stairway and a protected outdoor court on the roof.

Frank Gehry, Chiat Day Conference Room and Snake Chandelier, Santa Monica, California 1991

Eric Owen Moss, 8522 National Boulevard, Culver City, 1989–91

There is a wilful logic here, a pugnacious honesty turned sensuous. Like James Stirling, who would derive unlikely juxtapositions from requirements, Moss thrives on contradictory necessities. At the Lawson/Weston House in West Los Angeles he uses industrial vernacular forms in a quixotic way. The overall grey/green tonalities reconcile three different materials: concrete, metal and a special steel trowelled plaster he has developed. Roof, walls, floor all meld together in an angular, sculptural mass that seems to writhe and wrestle with itself. Then trussed wood and metal stringers break through – like punk jewellery – and a window, quite logically, rotates at the angle of the wall. On the inside, the stairway space is a fascinating light-box of reflected light and punched-through vistas, with industrial elements breaking through the white background at odd angles. Like Gehry's sculptural work, it is very idiosyncratic and at the same time thought through beautifully. In Los Angeles, architects have developed informality and dissonance into a very special art of *ekstasis* and the LA School has now influenced architecture in Japan, Britain and other parts of the world.

Eric Owen Moss,
Culver City
conversion/office, 1995

Eric Owen Moss,
Lawson/Weston
House, West Los
Angeles, 1988–93

THE ECSTASY OF THE ARCHITECTURAL IDEA
PETER EISENMAN AND DANIEL LIBESKIND

All great architects, in the end, are obsessed by architecture – otherwise they would not be first rate. This absorption in the medium constitutes the essence of the artistic sign. It is always, in part, self-referential, a sign which refers to its own plane of expression as part of the meaning. The concept sounds simple, but it was not until semiotics, the general theory of signs, was developed in the early part of the twentieth century that its importance was fully appreciated. All world-class architects construct a new virtual world which is internally related to the particular – even peculiar – plane of expression they set up. This is the pure architectural idea, the kernel of the building, its unique genetic instructions. Thus to fully appreciate any building one must grasp its conceptual blueprint: not the actual plans so much as the organisational concept which lies behind them.

More than any other designer, Peter Eisenman is motivated by the underlying architectural idea, its deep structure, its kernel. His Koizumi Lighting Theatre in Tokyo is generated by the shifted L-form. Eisenman sees the L, or El, as unstable, unfinished and disruptive and he likes it for these reasons. This may seem a little perverse, since architecture usually is commissioned for exactly the opposite reasons – to sit four-square on the ground, to embody a measure of permanence, psychic stability, even financial security. But Eisenman loves to question basic assumptions about architecture and life and that is precisely the point; he sets up his

Peter Eisenman, Koizumi Lighting Theatre, Tokyo, 1992, detail of window

Koizumi, lighting display floor, 3Ls

idiosyncratic world and its singular language, and then goes to work on it creating fantastic structures of the mind, and sensual structures which extend the idea of architecture. If one is offended by this, and some people are, then that is part of the experience: like much contemporary music, poetry, art and philosophy it is meant to repel as it attracts, meant to overturn assumptions as it invents new ones.

The L is not only disruptive but it moves out at the ends, because they are open, thus signifying 'unfinished'. Visually and conceptually the L spins or rotates on its elbow. Yet the functional virtue of the L is that it is part of a square, so it is easy to fabricate and fit into the ubiquitous grid. But therein lies the problem: the grid is the ultimate stable form and Eisenman ultimately strives for instability. So, in the land of earthquakes, he shifts and tilts the Ls against each other and layers them – blue, green and pink – as if the colours were different geological strata that had undergone seismic shift and the visitor wanted to find out what they were – sandstone, marble and granite. The deep structure of the solid L rotates conceptually through and around the whole building, shifted at a slight angle from the structural grid – which is the reference volume. It is hard to remember which colour of the triad is the frame of reference. Is that the point? After all, the General Theory of Relativity proved that there is no absolute fixed frame for the universe, no centre from which everything is expanding, no universal Mercator grid, no eternal

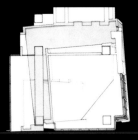

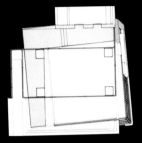

Peter Eisenman, floor plans of Koizumi Lighting Theatre, Tokyo, 1992

Door/corridor/spatial Ls interpenetrating

space–time coordinates. It is all
moving with respect to itself, tilting
and warping under gravity and
expansion. Whatever the case of
the universe, in this building the
shifted, layered planes are destabil-
ising and visually delightful. What
makes the building more than a
delight is the doggedness with which
the underlying idea is carried
through in the windows, doors,
walls, spaces and sections of the
building. This is architecture about
a new concept of itself.

Daniel Libeskind and the highly
creative engineer Cecil Balmond
have worked on another type of
dynamic open form: the chaotic
spiral. For the Victoria and Albert
Museum in London they propose a
new extension and entrance made
from six overlapping wall sections.
These fractal shapes, self-similar
cubes resembling an ice floe or
glacier, are actually derived from a
single load-bearing wall that spirals
upwards, holding itself! But it is not
the normal spiral of a snail or a
corkscrew. The point from which
the curves are generated moves
from one room to the next, and the
wall shapes are straight rather than
curved. But the ordering principle
of the 'chaotic spiral' determines
the jumps and is similar to the
details also.

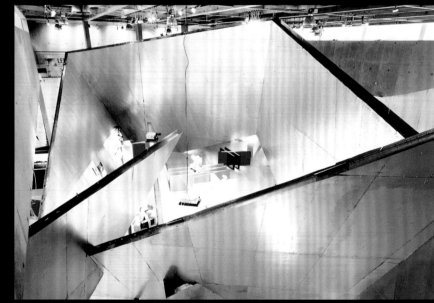

*Daniel Libeskind with
Cecil Balmond, engineer,
Victoria and Albert
extension proposal,
London, 1995–99*

*Exhibition at NAI,
Rotterdam, a mocked-
up version of the idea
of wall-spiral architec-
ture, 1997 (Courtesy
of NAI)*

These are 'fractiles', three tile forms which are related to each other and the whole set of angular shapes. Their enticing beauty, ever-renewing itself, stems from the fact that the overall pattern is continuously new yet always self-similar, just like the growth of an idea or a good conversation. Fractal order is the order of pleasurable experience. It is built into the nervous system, which must always have new stimuli, but with forms that are reasonably familiar. If exactly the same stimuli occur a nerve switches off, it will not fire again quickly; in contrast, if a completely chaotic set of stimuli occurs, no pattern will be perceived. So ecstatic experience, like perception in general, thrives on the ever-changing variations of a theme, here the chaotic spiral and its fractiles.

Perhaps all of this is not Ecstatic Architecture so much as the ecstasy of pure architectural ideas, taken to their beautiful, logical conclusion.

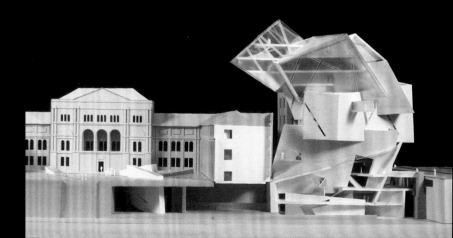

HARDCORE E — THE FETISHISTIC SUBLIME

If in kitsch and Camp 'nothing succeeds like excess', it is also true of a certain form of commercial ecstasy. Unity of mood, we have seen, characterises all types of ecstatic experience and so there is a natural tendency within the genre for an excessive emphasis on a few themes. When these themes are all directed at an obvious sexuality, and the one-liner of bodily gratification, we have Hardcore E, the Fetishistic Sublime. Nowhere is this more apparent than in the car and film industries.

A situation in which the two industries meet on shared ground is Roger Corman's *Wild Angels*. In the Movieland Wax Museum of Southern California one could find, in 1973, Nancy Sinatra immortalised as she jumped on to her palpitating chrome and polished black charger, with her white miniskirt pulled up forever above sparkling white leather boots. This determined teenage vixen was obviously the completion of the black supercharger, the machine's other half, and just in case male fantasies were flagging or too thick to get the point of the fetish, mirrors were conveniently located all around her – especially below.

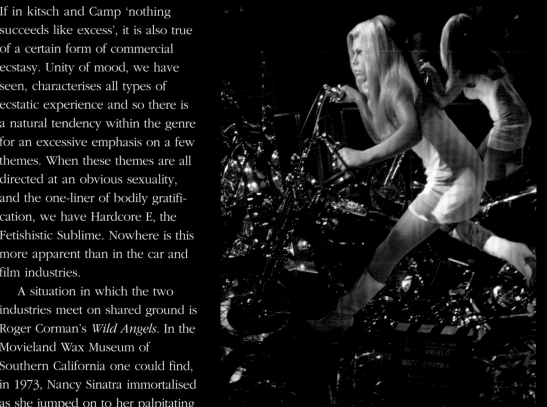

The Fetishistic Sublime, Nancy Sinatra in Wild Angels, *Movieland Wax Museum, Anaheim, California, 1973*

Sexual explicitness is often the joke at custom car fairs. How phallic can you make the exhaust pipes and cam shaft, how womb-like the interior? The humour of explicit metaphor extends across a range from eroticism to Camp, with such mad concoctions as the 'Rollswagon' (half Rolls, half Volkswagen) one of which combines the famous upfront radiator grill with a brothel interior. Another sensuous joke of 'Adhocism' is the His and Hers Bathtubmobile displayed at the Hollywood Motorama Museum. This uses luscious cream-studded padding as a contrast to the bath tub white. One drives sitting on a lavatory seat with toilet-paper rolls for bumpers and, as always, polished zoom-zoom exhausts (which are so ubiquitous they have probably ceased to have a phallic connotation).

His and Hers
Bathtubmobile,
(Courtesy of Hollywood
Motorama Museum,
Mike Roberts)

Sometimes such Hardcore E is allowed out on the street where it can frighten the drivers. The Bootmobile is an LA advertisement for 'quality shoes' making humorous use of the well-known fetish, while the 'Penismobile' (if that is its name) leaves little to the imagination (except what the garage looks like). In spite of being obvious one-liners, these works show a certain creative mapping: the formal simi-larities between car, foot and penis lead to clever comparisons of laces, glans and shoe-tread with the func-tional parts of a car and, finally, the exhaust is not a phallus (but rather the artery which serves it).

Much less imaginative, and straight hardcore, is the 'come-in' advertisement for exotic dancers which I came across in Houston, Texas in 1979. It is only the dancers' gargantuan dimensions and their juxtaposition with the scrubbed-white shack that give this a certain frisson and makes one laugh. Also, the too-obvious place-ment of the entrance door works because of the usual standards of Camp: 'it's so bad that it's good'.

'Penismobile', Los Angeles, 1973 (Photo courtesy Environmental Communications)

Following such recipes, Mr Madonna has created the Madonna Inn in San Luis Obispo out of a series of giant boulders that his earth-moving company has picked up over the years. These are composed into all sorts of strange and suggestive shapes, especially for the honeymooners who frequent the inn. A central fireplace is the understated torso of a very fat ladyman with bulging muscles and *mons veneris* – or something like that.

Entertainment Architecture, Disney's sobriquet since the mid-1980s for its building policy, never usually manages to attain the energy of Hardcore E because it is aimed at a midcult audience. The rough edges are gone, the wildness of cowboy capitalism is absent in this architecture of total control.

Michael Graves' Dolphin Hotel in Orlando, Florida is good taste megalomania, a Ledoux pyramid in Graves-green set off by holiday pinstripes, jumped-up urns and sub-Bernini dolphins, the kind of gestural icon built all over South East Asia before the collapse of the Tiger economies. This sort of architecture really ought to be ecstatic, given its explicit intent to arouse and amaze, but the corporate theming keeps it safely surrounded by the ring fence of stereotype. Ecstasy can only be really ecstatic when it shatters taboo in a frenzy of delight.

Madonna Inn fireplace, San Luis Obispo California, 1974

Michael Graves, Dolphin Hotel, Disneyworld, Orlando, Florida, 1988

BREATHLESS — THE FLYING CANTILEVER

The normal experience of ecstasy, if such a thing exists, is described as a sense of effortless floating in space, a sublime weightlessness. Unless one is underwater or an astronaut in outer space, gravity asserts its heavy presence; unless one is in sexual ecstasy or in an hallucinatory state, bodily weight pervades consciousness. Architecture, especially concrete architecture, is a strong expression of mass and that is why, in the twentieth century, it is something of a paradox that anti-gravitational architecture should have become such a recurrent theme, even in concrete. The oxymoron 'light/heaviness' is the result. El Lissitzky's Sky-hook project of 1924 typifies the genre. Asymmetrically placed horizontal offices, about fourteen storeys off the ground, are stretched way out from their cores into space – cerebral diving boards, flying cantilevers.

This idea has been in the back of architects' minds ever since then, reaching fruition with Philip Johnson's building at the 1964 World's Fair and, today, with the work of Zaha Hadid and Rem Koolhaas. The flying cantilever also has become a metaphor literalised, especially in the large airplane such as the Boeing 747. When one looks out at the sleek metallic forms sliding over the clouds, one recalls the famous cosmic sentiments which the revolutionary architect Ledoux expressed two hundred years ago: 'There is architecture up among the whirlwinds and clouds that battle to dominate the sky'. Lissitzky's Sky-hook, the skyscraper, and so many

TWA over the Arctic

Frank Lloyd Wright,
George Sturges House,
Brentwood, Los
Angeles, 1939

of Frank Lloyd Wright's cantilevered schemes, perched on Los-Angeles' hillsides, all address the blueness of the sky. It is the backdrop and challenge for flying, now after fifty years of building against the laws of gravity on the side of sliding hills, a hopeful Californian dream. The cantilever aspires to walk on air and, functionally, it provides the shelter for open-air living, the reason many people move to California.

Zaha Hadid, in the early 1980s, derived from the cantilever a grammar of flying beams. Her project for the Peak in Hong Kong took the rocky outcrops of the site as a basic metaphor, polished them into overlapping rectangles, like shards of rock exploding along lines of force. This 'Planetary', or 'Anti-Gravitational Architecture', was built at Vitra but with more acute angles. Again the dichotomy light/heaviness of the flying concrete defies expectation, just as the anamorphic distortions defy perspective. By stretching laws of nature and perception Hadid, like the Constructivists, celebrates cosmic elements at a basic level. John Denton, in Australia, has expanded this approach on a gigantic scale and made an entire conference centre take flight.

The aerial metaphor is also never far away from the constructions of high-tech architects, but they dissolve the surface in a filigree of webs, hanging glass and exoskeleton. Richard Rogers, both at the Lloyd's of London gateway and the Channel Four Headquarters, creates the most airy entry canopies ever made. At Lloyd's the canopy

Zaha Hadid, Vitra Fire Station, Weil am Rhein, 1993

John Denton, Conference Centre, Melbourne, 1996

soars out from a heavy background, above the ermine and red robes of the doormen, like a transparent pterodactyl trying to flap its wings. The number of working drawings – of joints, bolts and cross-braces – must exceed that for a small house. This diaphanous architecture comes as close to magical suspension as it ever gets.

Kazuo Shinohara, on the other hand, celebrates the solidity of the Boeing 747, its massive power as an aluminium volume. In Tokyo he bisects a hall, at the top, with a half-round wing of a plane, or per-haps it is more like a fuselage. This enigmatic form, which is used as a restaurant, juts way out at both ends becoming a double cantilever, and this takes us back to a funda-mental structural principle which was explored at the beginning of the century. Like a seesaw, the cantilever makes sense if it balances weight at opposite ends. Le Corbusier often employed it in this rational way and, so used, it can actually lessen some structural dimensions, thus reducing cost. This depends on what takes the structural forces, the forces of bending and the moment of inertia; the column or the beam?

Rem Koolhaas has exploited these rational and expressive ques-tions for their odd contradictions and unlikely poetry. In a house in Paris, the Villa Dall'Ava, he takes ribbon-window volumes and pro-jects them over space, as did Lissitzky, but their balance is not what one would expect. One cubic volume is supported in the middle and therefore has to be pulled

Richard Rogers and Partners, Lloyd's of London, entrance canopy, 1986

Kazuo Shinohara, Tokyo Institute of Technology Centennial Hall, Tokyo, 1987–88

down on one side, so it can hover on the other. Because we expect the Corbusian volume to be supported regularly by a rational grid, we infer the missing columns, look for them and ask, 'Who forgot to put them in?' That is the oddity, and we are forced to observe it because the conventions are so strong. Koolhaas uses one convention of rationality, the seesaw cantilever, against another, the Corbusier cube set on pilotis (but without its pilotis) and the result is neither the euphoria of flying nor the excitement of anti-gravitation: it is the ecstasy of anti-logic logic, paradox squared.

His House in Bordeaux pushes this asymmetrical balance even further, as the drawing makes clear. Here an a-centred core and cross-beam hold up the main structure, an inhabitable flying beam cantilevered at both ends. The long ends extend about equally, the see-saw is in balance. But there is something strange if one looks closer. Because, on the short sides the supports are a-centric, there is a tendency for the box to tip over, so a counterweight cube is hung off the side like a giant pendulum. Dynamic, asymmetrical balance? The moving building? Wilful logic, perplexity? Whatever the case, the cantilever flies on all sides and spreads its wings for the ultimate in *plein-air* living. Californians, eat your heart out, drink Claret.

Rem Koolhaas, Villa Dall'Ava, Paris, cantilevered ribbon-windows

Rem Koolhaas, structural diagram and House in Bordeaux, 1994–98

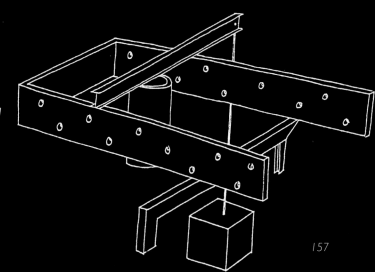

Cyberspace *Maggie Toy*

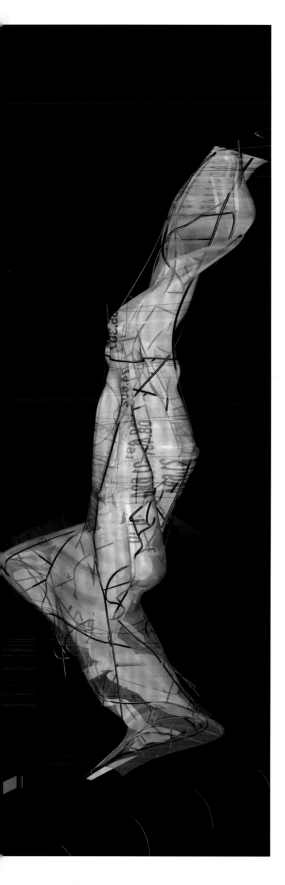

Cyberspace is a habitat for the imagination, a place where the ecstatic imagination is encouraged to reach optimum levels. Cyber is a residual term from early systems analysis and one appropriated by almost any condition that enlists the aid of a microprocessor at the service of some otherwise articulated human activity. The term 'Cyberspace' was first coined by William Gibson in his science fiction novel *Neuromancer* in the early 1980s. It was soon adopted by the architectural cognoscenti, although the architectural possibilities of the field were being investigated well before the term evolved in popular consciousness.

The comprehension of the virtual world's relevance within the real world is difficult to address definitively, but there can be no doubt that the medium facilitates a unique creative freedom. In Cyberspace an artificial world exists which is no longer subject to the usual laws of physics; visual impressions of navigating through rooms, of flying and floating away from the restrictions of gravity can be contrived as a matter of course. Within the Cyber environment, architecture can be completely 'liquid' as Marcos Novak argues: 'it is an architecture that is no longer satisfied with only space and form and light and all the aspects of the real world. It is

an architecture of fluctuating relations between abstract elements.'

The construction of this type of world walks the inspirational tightrope between excitement and terror: arguably a perfect state for endless invention. Ceasing to impose conceptions of physical reality upon those of virtual reality, it begins to demonstrate the possibilities with greater clarity and is the first step into the demanding world of cyber design; in making this step the relation between this and ecstatic design becomes increasingly apparent.

Although creative inspirations are 'reality oriented' and objective in viewpoint, they do not pertain to reality. At the time of creative inspiration, proposed creative projects are still speculative mental constructs. In this sense, the comprehensive understanding and use of the technology supplied by computer systems can provide the ideal vehicle for the ecstatic imagination.

An hallucination has been defined as 'an apparent perception of an external object when no such object is present'. This definition could also be applied to many of the images shown here. The creative minds that made them available to us may well have been inspired by the drug culture in which we now exist.

Nox Architects/Lars
Spuybroek, Beachness

Beachness, hotel interior

These images demonstrate the design for a boulevard and beach hotel in Noordwijk, The Netherlands, commissioned by the Amsterdam Design Institute. Beachness is designed as a certain state of mobility, because the beach should be conceived primarily as a field in which everything is in a state of openness and non-fixation.

The Vortex 2000 project is for a period of intense acceleration of global activity and connectivity in which the powerful currents of our technologically augmented society have combined to expand areas for new human experience and perception, while blurring the once perceived separation between a virtual reality and the physical world.

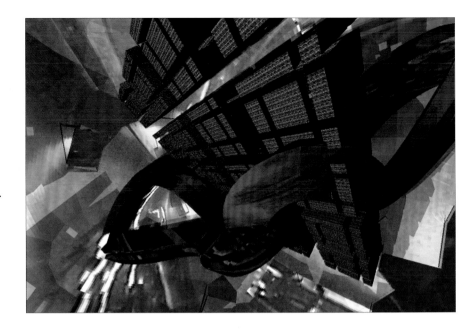

Located at the eastern end of Wall Street, the Cultural Information Exchange Center was designed as a temporary structure. The small scale of the site posed the challenge of designing a structure that would not be eclipsed by the monumental scale of the surrounding buildings. The building was perceived as a flow of bodies and information through space over time

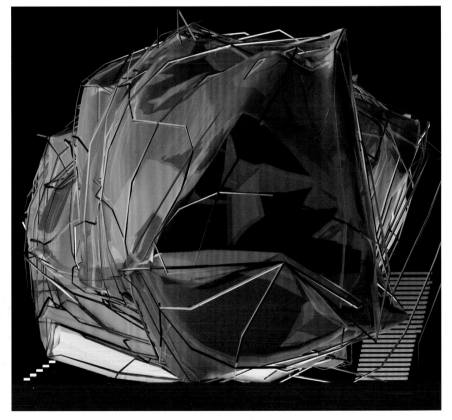

Christopher Romero,
Vortex 2000

Ammar Eloueini,
Cultural Information
Exchange Center, New
York City

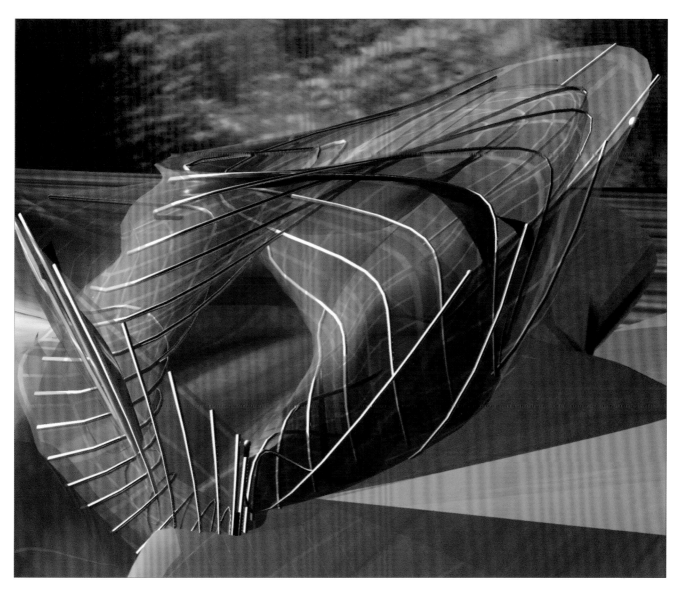

An investigation into contemporary domesticity to reconsider dwelling for the next millennium, the Möbius House is neither an interior space nor exterior form. It is a transferable membrane that reconfigures binary notions of interior/ exterior into a continuous, interwrapping median – it is a hypersurface.

Stephen Perrella with Rebecca Carpenter, the Möbius House study

'The synthesis of energy, matter and information into a three-parameter system of explanation has created conditions that allow us to think the unthinkable and extend our imagination to the limits of the conceivable.'

Karl S Chu, Phylux

Karl S Chu, Phylogon I

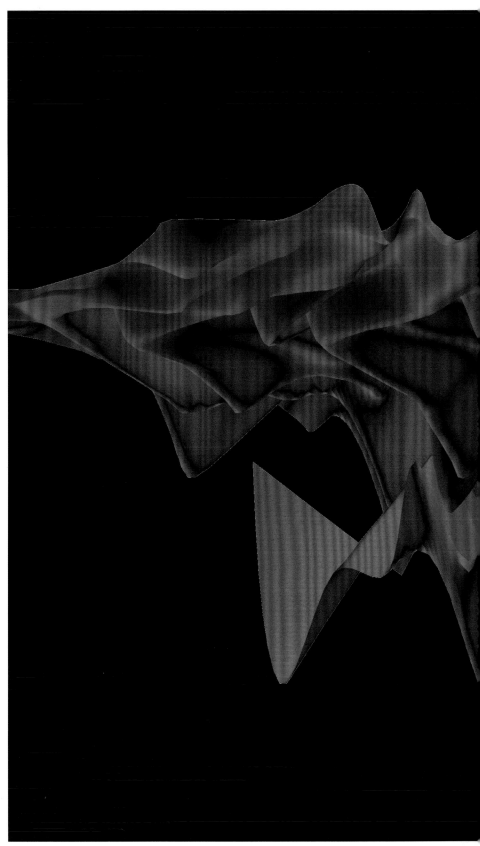

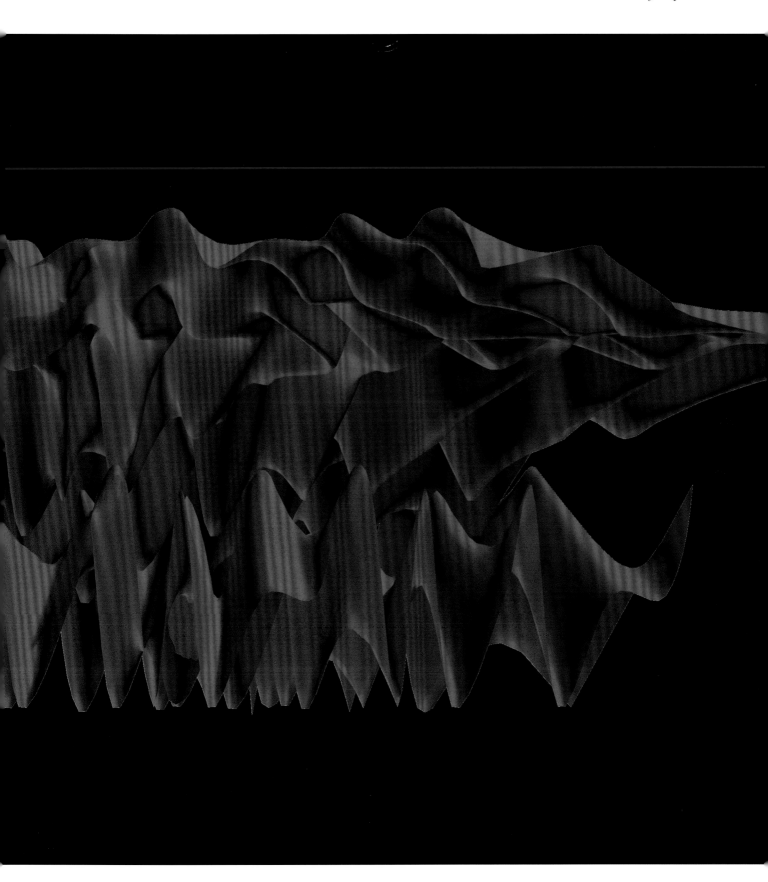

'Eversion, as the name implies, is the turning inside-out of virtuality, so that it is no longer contained in the technologies that support it but is cast into our midst and projected onto our architectures and into our cities. If screens are related how we understand the interval between conceivable and presentable and transmodernity urges this interval forwards to the zone of transmutations and transfigurations, then everted screens become instruments by which to glimpse and enact that which is barely within perceptual or conceptual reach.'

Marcos Novak,
investigations into
the Paracube

Marcos Novak,
Warp Map

'Liquid architecture is not the mimesis of natural fluids in architecture. First and foremost it is a liquefying of everything that has traditionally been crystalline and solid in architecture. It is the contamination of media. This pavilion has been seized by the concept of the liquid. Not only in its shape and use of materials but in its interior environment it tries to effect a prototypical merging of hardware, software and wetware.'

Nox Architects/Lars Spuybroek, Fresh Water Pavilion, The Netherlands

Bilbaoism –The Unreasonable Effectiveness of Sensuous Knowledge
Charles Jencks

Few buildings have had the impact of Frank Gehry's Guggenheim Museum, in Bilbao. In a time of media hype it has been called, more than once, the building of the century, leaving barely two years to a competitor. This acclaim might stem from its presence, both in the city and mountain landscape. Le Corbusier's pilgrimage church at Ronchamp and Jørn Utzon's Sydney Opera House achieved similar notoriety in the sixties and seventies because they, too, were made from curved and unusual shapes, but particularly because they took command of their landscapes with similar power. The incredible urban presence has led to overstated metaphors rolling off the press: an explosion of light, a starburst of energy, unstoppable white lava, overlapping waves, fish thrashing, a Constructivist artichoke or, most ecstatic of all, a shiny sequinned swimmer about to burst out of her bathing suit. Metaphors are a 'carrying over' from one idea to another, a transgression, a metamorphosis of categories and they go to the heart of the erotic and ecstatic. As we have seen, Ecstatic Architecture typically crosses boundaries, merges categories and concentrates on itself – its own internal world.

Bilbaoism is a term I would use to describe both the extreme emphasis on architecture about itself and the extremity of response to this, but it is worth focusing on the positive reactions for a moment because they are so unusual in their unanimity, particularly among architects. They, like all professionals, are usually a jealous lot. At the opening of the museum in October 1997, and before, I was struck by how many architects of different persuasions had made the trip to Bilbao and were profoundly impressed. One, Eric Moss, who has developed his own highly expressive system, said the building was so good that it blocked off this way forward: improvement along this avenue seemed impossible. Architects respond implicitly to the extreme self-referentiality that works, architecture squared.

The New Guggenheim in its pivotal site – at the juncture between a river, highway, industrial landscape, the city and nature

THE REBIRTH OF THE URBAN MONUMENT

Almost everyone is struck by the way the museum building captures and uses the site. Frank Gehry actually chose the exposed position, at the slight bend in the Nervion River; a difficult point because it was the juncture between opposite urban pressures: disused naval docks, railroad yards, a highway bridge with four lanes of traffic, the medieval fragments of the city and its heavy, nineteenth-century gridded Classicism. Above all, the large hills flow down to what was this mess, and it must have been these visual lines, and the heterogeneity itself, which led Gehry to the choice of location. In any case, placing the building where he did gave it the pivotal position in the city and countryside, like occupying the centre of a chessboard with the queen. No other building in Bilbao can beat this position, it is the final move in the end-game of the city.

When one looks down on Gehry's silvery eruptions glowing against the dark masonry background of Bilbao, one is reminded of Chartres Cathedral proclaiming itself in the landscape and city, or the *palazzo publico* commanding the piazza in Siena. The twentieth century has produced many failed monuments, and the anti-monuments which are skyscrapers, and this is one of the first, recent urban monuments to be convincing. Coincidentally, it also epitomises a trend which has been underway for thirty years – the museum as cathedral. When the new Guggenheim is seen either from the surrounding hills, or from between the canyon walls of the nineteenth-century classical city, it appears like a steel-clad Notre Dame, the anchor to the whole urban fabric – its focus, the place to be, the heart of downtown.

The fact that art is worshipped inside, and that it is by those such as Richard Serra, Julian Schnabel and Jeff Koons, may offend some and not a few Basques, who wonder why they should pay to house the lend-lease programme of New York's Guggenheim Museum. But these questions of art replacing religion and an imperial art of America dominating the local culture are becoming marginal as the citizens begin to see the trade-off work. They have one of the great monuments of the 1990s which might give Bilbao a European presence, might regenerate a declining industrial city and, along with other buildings by important architects such as Foster and Calatrava, give the city new confidence. This is why the bargain was made with the Guggenheim in the first place.

The Long Gallery with Richard Serra's Snake *and Lawrence Wiener's* REDUCED *below the Gehry assemblage of flying beams, lighting catwalks and light scoops*

Crudely put, it was the gamble to see if culture could replace ship-building; art and leisure industries take the place of rust-belt manufacture, an experiment which has been tried in other cities with mixed results. It will take three or four years to see if this experiment works. As for the art chosen for the opening exhibit, some of it is bombastic and inflated, especially Lawrence Wiener's much expanded REDUCED, which climbs twenty-five feet up a wall. But the new Guggenheim answers a contemporary problem. However inadequate art is as a religion, however much artists and architects object to the monument, the large museum is perhaps the best public focus we have found this century. It may not provide a true or complete public realm, but it is the only one we have been able to invest with the prestige, money, and creativity of the old great monuments.

THE NEW PARADIGM – NATURE'S CHANGING EROTICISM

Yet there is an entirely different reason for the new Guggenheim's importance: its key place in an emergent tradition. Along with Daniel Libeskind's Jewish Museum in Berlin and Peter Eisenman's school of architecture in Cincinnati, it is a building which confirms the new paradigm of what could be called Complexity Architecture, or Nonlinear Architecture (after the new sciences of complexity and nonlinearity). This confirmation of a change is the reason it is so interesting to the architectural profession. It extends ideas which are at the edge of knowledge, and knowledge, as the Bible states, can be erotic, dangerous and forbidden – a sin.

The idea that has attracted the attention of both architects and the public is the notion that buildings can get closer to nature in its infinite variety, become less boring, less predictable, more dynamic – at little extra cost. One of the leading sciences of complexity was formulated by Benoit Mandelbrot in *The Fractal Geometry of Nature* (1977). Here, he argues that nature is not made, as most Westerners from Plato to Cézanne and Modern architects believed, from absolute geometric figures – the cone, sphere and cylinder. These are exceptions, not the prevalent underlying patterns. The sun, planetary rotation and the near straight line of a bullet were the few things that exhibited Platonic form and, although architecture has been based on primary shapes since the Egyptians first started with pyramids and squares, nature is not normally Euclidean. The tree, the fern, the lightning bolt, the coastline of Scotland – to cite Mandelbrot's favourite

Entrance side: 'Classical' galleries to the left, petal shape forms to the right, called 'Nemo' and 'Zorro' and descent into the atrium, straight ahead

examples – are fractals, irregular fractured forms that have a dynamic mixture of order and chaos known as self-similarity.

One can see this quality in Gehry's petal-forms, the twenty-six or so self-similar flower shapes that erupt over the masonry boxes, much like a zealous plant sprouts over a window box. This self-similarity should be contrasted with Modernism's self-sameness; the fact that in any curtain wall of Mies van der Rohe all the windows are exactly the same. By contrast, nature is always slightly changing the size and shape of every leaf on a branch, or wave on the sea. Gehry also uses a family of forms and twists, each one a little differently. For the contractors constructing a fluid architecture, this non-Euclidean geometry can be disorienting. Each petal had to be given a name, such as 'Cobra', 'Fish', 'Boot', 'Potemkin' and 'Zorro',

Atrium, 160 feet of flying bridges, white swirls and dark steel

so the builders could easily refer to where they were and the distinctiveness of each shape. The names locate and eroticise a place.

The entrance descends into the museum, an interesting contrast to the usual raised entry, and to the right of the steps is a svelte 'whale' – or some metaphor of life. Fractal shapes immediately recall a basic fact of nature: it is always changing, always interesting, always provoking a response. The question is whether, given the costs of varying each unit, architecture can be as lively.

These fluid fractals were designed partly by computer. After many modelled studies, they were systematised in three dimensions by a French computer program, Catia, which had been developed to economise the complex curves of the Mirage fighter. This program translated the forms into the most economical cutting of the interior structure and exterior surface. Hence, the Nonlinear Architecture of self-similarity became competitive with Modernist architecture of self-sameness: according to the local architects who built it, the fractal curves only added ten to fifteen per cent to the basic costs.

There is one inconsistency in the design. The endless, titanium panels are unvarying – self-same – and a little like wallpaper as a result. A deeper Nonlinear Architecture would be self-similar throughout. Apparently, however, that would have added considerable cost, because every titanium sheet had to be pre-bent for an exact role. Hence this building is a stage in the developing paradigm, a step before the surface is finally worked out as a variable pattern. It is only a matter of time before architects achieve the sophisticated variation of the reptile's hide, the snake's skin or the fish's scale – all of which gently change as the surface goes around a complex curve. I was very surprised that Gehry did not push for this solution, especially because he had shown the way with his Fish and Snake Lights of the 1980s.

In any case, the building heightens the experience of art by drawing people into a drama of surprise and sensuality. It reaches out to every angle and view, it ducks under a nearby freeway in order to sprout another exuberant entrance. And yet however rich in spatial ambiguities, the ordering idea is never lost. Orientation is around the large atrium space, the heart of the museum to which one always returns, and this fans out to the river and a fantastic view of the mountains. The drama is created by

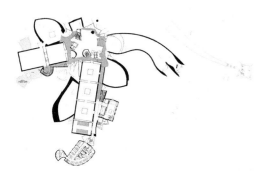

Plan showing the contrast of grammars: square masonry, angular glass and titanium curves

strong contrast. White curves are sliced by dark metal and glass and some flying bridges that jump the atrium space. Opposed to all this architectural movement are the surrounding hillsides, which can be glimpsed through the swirls. Because the shapes are fractals and self-similar, they take on an inevitability, a logic which one accepts. At some places the exterior titanium skin folds into the building and becomes a continuity between the outside and inside.

When I first saw the museum without the art installed, I felt there were two main problems with the interior galleries: too much background white – white walls everywhere – and, on the upper floors, a sense of claustrophobia caused by closing off the centre of spaces with high walls, so that natural light could go to the floors below. However, when the spaces were full of people and art on the opening night, I experienced these aspects quite differently. The smaller galleries at the top house the 'old' Modern art, that of the 1920s, and they provided a very appropriate scale for these smaller paintings and sculptures. With a wry historical irony the works by Klee and Kandinsky, and the galleries enclosing them, are called 'classical' – such is the way the big brash new art reclassifies and upstages the old. 'Inside the White Cube' was a very influential article of the 1970s, by Brian O'Doherty, which describes the Modernist convention of display that has dominated the twentieth century. This method decontextualises art, puts it on an abstract pedestal, as if it were a religious icon to be worshipped for itself. The logic is fitting for abstract and spiritual works, such as those of the early Bauhaus, but when white cubes take over all the art a strange distancing takes place. Aesthetic experience is enforced on every piece, even that which has a political or social or historical message. The New Guggenheim follows this convention for the most part, yet there are a few rooms, such as the one in which Francesco Clemente painted site-specific works, where the convention is broken. These exceptions thus suggest a more inclusive attitude towards art and mark the museum as a modest step in the direction of pluralism.

Gehry challenges rather than overthrows Modernism, and in this mixed attitude he may be perceived as the typical Post-Modernist. Most of his galleries are right-angled, but they all possess certain elements – such as the lighting catwalks and unusual proportions– which displace the neutrality of the White Cube. The spaces were also studied and modelled

Pinched corners, like pleats in fabric or the arrises of a Doric column, sculpt the light and define the movement of each volume

endlessly, so each one feels quite unique. Through the study models Gehry began to see that the top galleries could extend towards the light, like phototropic plants following the path of the sun. This reaching towards light and energy is part of the petal grammar and it is ultimately what gives the building its quality, its depth as a work of art. On the outside, each petal is, in effect, an off-square space with a pinched corner. This grammar, which Gehry initiated in 1987 with the Vitra commissions, has been improved here by the addition of delicate fillets which sculpt light and define the movement of each volume towards a sharp edge. These clear lines, like the pleats on a trouser leg, are also like the arrises on a Doric column – expressive refinements which lead the eye upwards. They also allow the hyperbolic curves to move more freely in any direction.

Thus the building as a whole is innovative, both as a new form of fluidity, a new fractal grammar, and as the modification of a Modernist museum convention. Its progress in developing both an aesthetic and a new way of doing things is part of the broader search for a new paradigm of Complexity Architecture, the understanding of a new potential for architecture. This is why the Bilbao Guggenheim is the building of the moment; both profession and public learn from it while enjoying sensual pleasures. In effect its strength comes from combining two powerful instincts, the drive to know more about the universe and to relate to it aesthetically, erotically, mentally. Curiously, given the importance of this double drive, there is no term for it. What should we call the impact, which the Modernists themselves began to explore: Cognirotic? Sensuolect? Erocinate? These do not work, but the New Guggenheim shows we do need a word for the synergetic combination of aesthetic delight and new knowledge. This is something that was not anticipated in the Modern era when reason and emotion were juxtaposed as opposites. But the brain is an extension of nature, like everything else, and has to respond to opposite drives and qualities. It makes a trade-off, balancing the validities of sensuality and reason in some form of calculus. What happens when these antinomies point in the same direction? Surprise, delight, the reconciliation of habitually divided territories, the consummation of sex. Ecstatic Architecture is always about joining that which has hitherto been separate; a dislocation, an insane rapture at seeing extremes which miraculously touch.

Index